THE SIERRA CLUB GUIDE TO THE
ANCIENT FORESTS OF THE NORTHEAST

The Sierra Club Guide to the ANCIENT FORESTS of the NORTHEAST

BRUCE KERSHNER

ROBERT T. LEVERETT

SIERRA CLUB BOOKS

SAN FRANCISCO

Text copyright © 2004 by Bruce Kershner and Robert T. Leverett
Maps copyright ©2004 by Sierra Club

Published by Sierra Club Books
85 Second Street, San Francisco, CA 94105
www.sierraclub.org/books

Produced and distributed by
University of California Press
Berkeley, California
University of California Press, Ltd.
London, England
www.ucpress.edu

SIERRA CLUB, SIERRA CLUB BOOKS, and the Sierra Club design logos
are registered trademarks of the Sierra Club.

Library of Congress Cataloging-in-Publication Data
    Kershner, Bruce
The Sierra Club guide to the ancient forests of the northeast / Bruce Kershner
and Robert T. Leverett.
    p.   cm.
    Includes index.
    ISBN 1-57805-066-9
    1. Old growth forests—Northeastern States—Guidebooks. 2. Northeastern
States—Guidebooks. I. Title: Guide to the ancient forests of the northeast.
II. Leverett, Robert T., 1941 – III. Sierra Club. IV. Title.
    SD387.043K47 2004
    333.75'0974—dc21   2003053005

Book and cover design by Blue Design
First Edition
08 07 06 05 04
10 9 8 7 6 5 4 3 2 1

*This book is dedicated to the Native Americans
who once inhabited the great forests of the Northeast
and to today's Americans who are committed to
protecting the last ancient forests
so that future generations can enjoy them.*

Contents

Western Pennsylvania *(see map, page 1)*   39

Eastern Pennsylvania *(see map, page 2)*   59

New Jersey *(see map, page 3)*

Western New York and the Finger Lakes Region *(see map, page 4)*

New York's Adirondack Mountains *(see map, page 5)*

Hudson River Valley and New York Metro Area *(see map, page 6)*

Connecticut *(see map, page 8)* and Rhode Island *(see map, page 9)*

Massachusetts *(see map, page 10)*

Vermont *(see map, page 11)*

New Hampshire *(see map, page 12)* 235

Maine *(see map, page 13)* 247

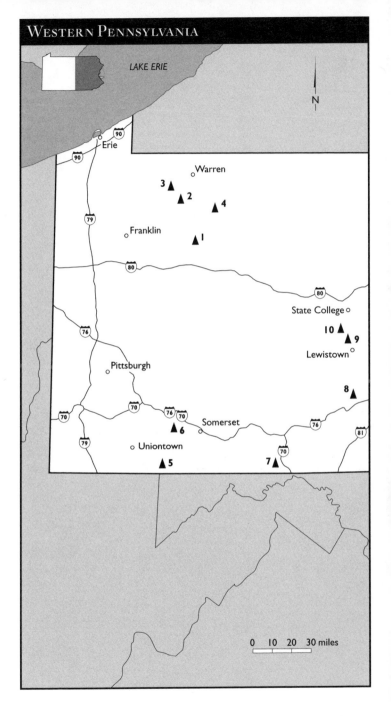

WESTERN PENNSYLVANIA

LAKE ERIE

N

Erie

Warren

3
2
4

Franklin

1

State College

10
9

Lewistown

Pittsburgh

8

Somerset

6

Uniontown

5

7

0   10   20   30 miles

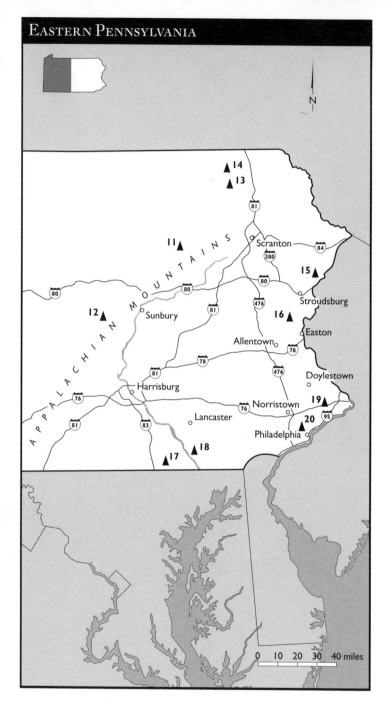

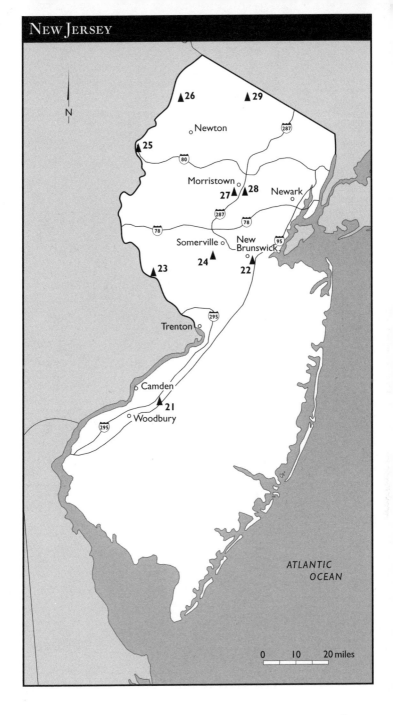

N

▲26   ▲29

○ Newton

287

▲25

80

Morristown ○
27 ▲ ▲ 28   Newark ○

287

78

78

○ Somerville   New
Brunswick
24 ▲   95
22 ▲

▲23

295

Trenton ○

○ Camden
▲ 21

295   ○ Woodbury

ATLANTIC
OCEAN

0   10   20 miles

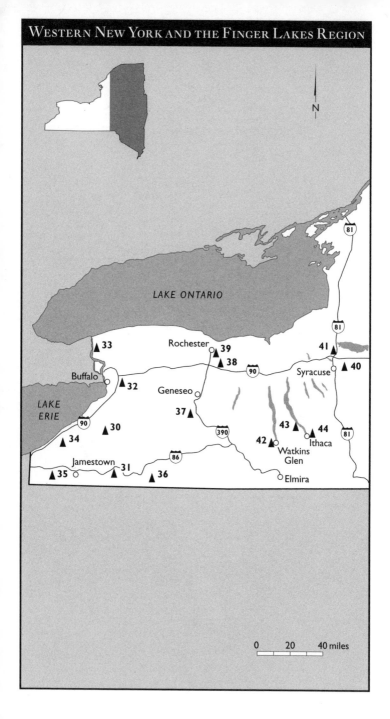

NEW YORK'S ADIRONDACK MOUNTAINS

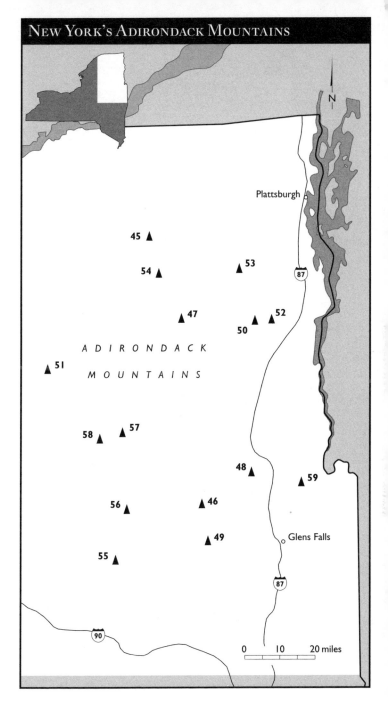

Plattsburgh

87

45 ▲

54 ▲

53 ▲

47 ▲

52 ▲
50 ▲

A D I R O N D A C K

▲ 51

M O U N T A I N S

58 ▲   ▲ 57

48 ▲

▲ 59

56 ▲   ▲ 46

49 ▲

Glens Falls

55 ▲

87

0   10   20 miles

90

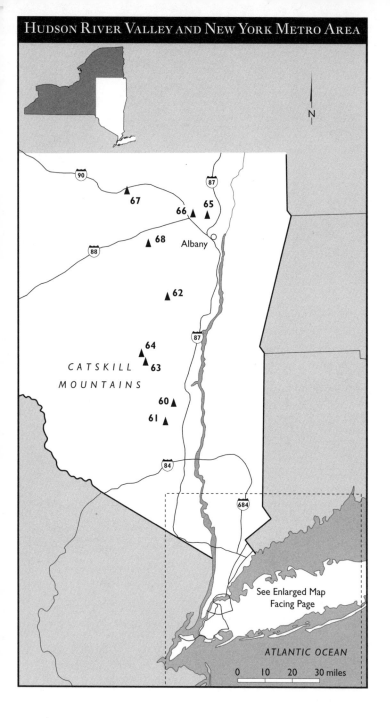

N

90

87

67

66 65

88

68

Albany

62

87

64

63

CATSKILL

MOUNTAINS

60

61

84

684

See Enlarged Map
Facing Page

ATLANTIC OCEAN

0   10   20   30 miles

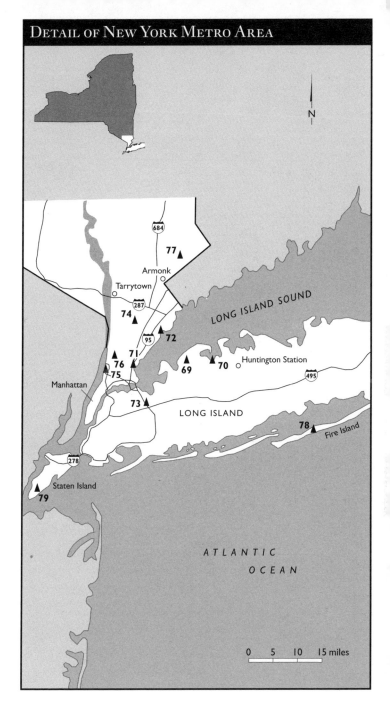

N

684

77

Armonk

Tarrytown

287

74

95

72

LONG ISLAND SOUND

71

76

69

70

Huntington Station

75

495

Manhattan

73

LONG ISLAND

78

Fire Island

278

79

Staten Island

ATLANTIC

OCEAN

0   5   10   15 miles

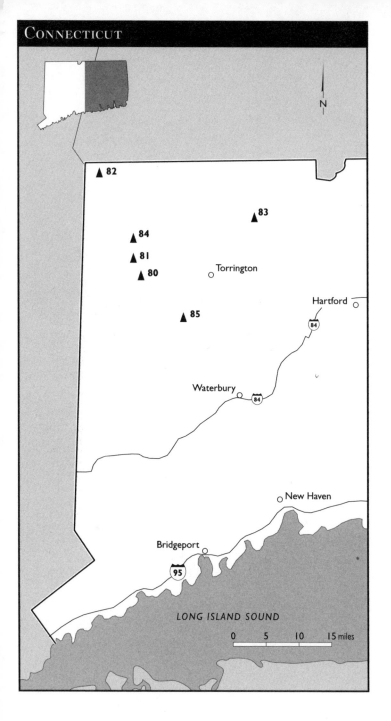

N

▲ 82

▲ 83

▲ 84

▲ 81

▲ 80

○ Torrington

Hartford ○

84

▲ 85

Waterbury ○

84

New Haven ○

Bridgeport ○

95

LONG ISLAND SOUND

0   5   10   15 miles

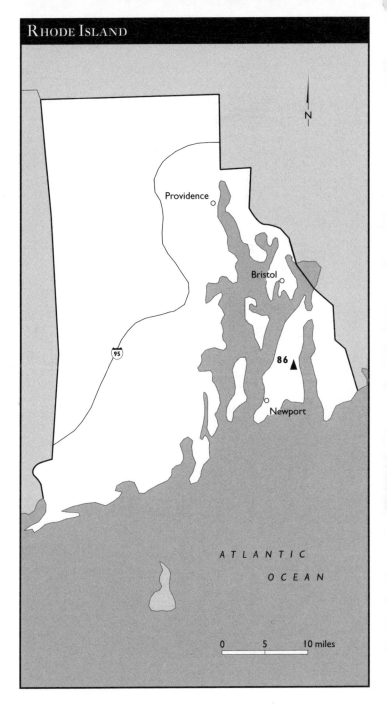

N

Providence

Bristol

86 ▲

Newport

95

A T L A N T I C

O C E A N

0   5   10 miles

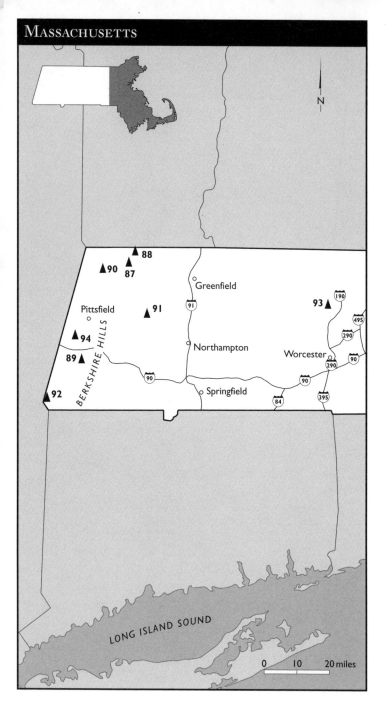

MASSACHUSETTS

N

Greenfield

91

▲ 88
▲ 90 ▲ 87

Pittsfield

▲ 91

93 ▲   190

495

290

▲ 94

89 ▲

Northampton   Worcester   90

290

92 ▲

90

BERKSHIRE HILLS

90   Springfield   90

84   395

LONG ISLAND SOUND

0   10   20 miles

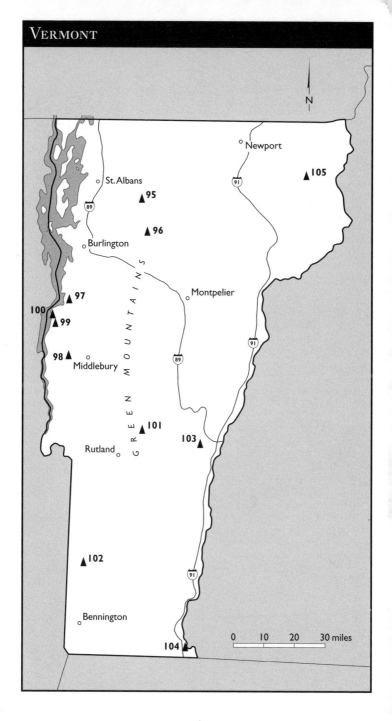

○ Newport

▲105

○ St. Albans

▲95

89

▲96

○ Burlington

▲97

100 ▲99

98 ▲

○ Middlebury

G R E E N   M O U N T A I N S

Montpelier ○

91

89

▲101

103 ▲

Rutland ○

▲102

91

Bennington ○

104 ▲

| 0 | 10 | 20 | 30 miles |

N

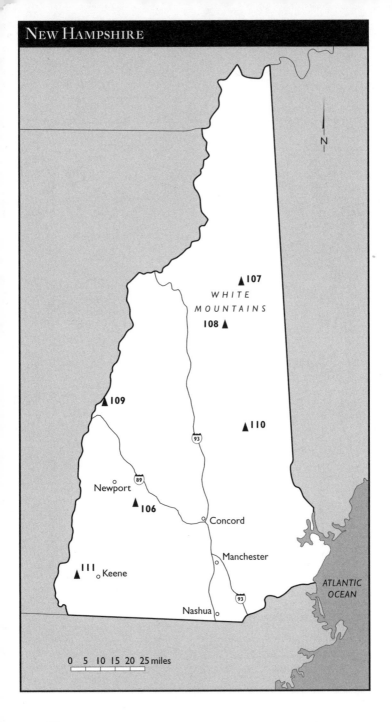

▲107

*WHITE
MOUNTAINS*

108 ▲

▲109

▲110

93

89

○ Newport

▲106

○ Concord

Manchester
○

▲111 ○ Keene

93

Nashua ○

0 5 10 15 20 25 miles

N

ATLANTIC
OCEAN

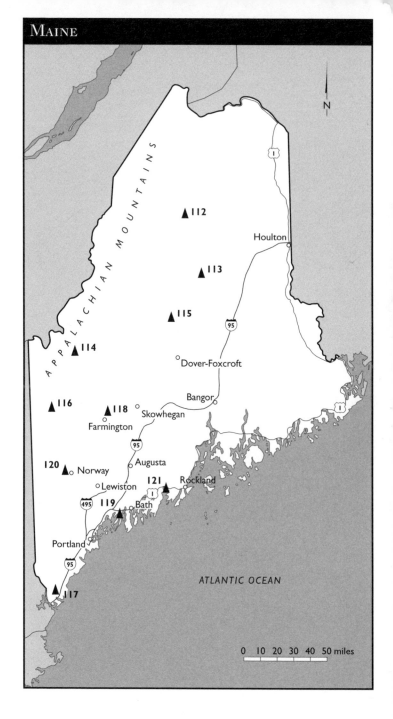

Preface

The natural landscape of the eastern United States has been thoroughly explored over the past four centuries. All of the region's peaks have been measured, its rivers and lakes have been mapped, and all but the tiniest of its living organisms have been identified. By the early nineteenth century, the era for new discoveries appeared to have ended.

Until recently, however, a hidden treasure was yet to be discovered: old-growth forests. Most experts believed that ancient forests in the eastern part of the country had been all but destroyed by centuries of exploitation. But beginning in the 1980s, a group of modern-day explorers—from "ordinary" nature lovers to trained professionals—teamed up to look for these presettlement woods.

What they found has astounded everybody: hundreds of thousands of acres of ancient forest that no one knew existed, some of it near or even within cities—including a stand in Manhattan. Among the first of the survey teams were those started in the early 1980s in Massachusetts and western New York by the authors of this book. They resulted in the most complete old-growth surveys, with discovery or confirmation of more than 120 ancient forests so far. Other teams in such places as the southern Appalachians and the Ozarks searched for and discovered their own old growth.

At first, these old-growth hunters were largely unaware of each other's work. But two developments changed that, encouraging these individuals to form a collective movement. In 1993, conservationist and director of the Eastern Old Growth Clearinghouse Mary Byrd Davis completed a groundbreaking inventory of all known eastern ancient forests. Her book *Old Growth in the East: A Survey* (Wild Earth Publications) gave the nation its first look at where and how much old growth had survived in the eastern United States.

During the same period, this book's coauthor Robert Leverett launched an annual series of Eastern Old Growth conferences from Arkansas to New England. For the first time, scientists, forest managers, public officials, activists, writers, artists, and philosophers could directly pool knowledge and plan research. These meetings brought public attention to the primeval stands that were still threatened by logging and development. Meanwhile, coauthor Bruce Kershner further raised the public's awareness by helping to organize independent campaigns that successfully prevented logging of a number of large stands of old growth in four northeastern states.

This book goes one more step; its purpose is to introduce the public to the splendor of the remaining old-growth forests in the Northeast. The sites featured in this book are not the cut-over woodlands that most Americans living in the eastern part of the country have come to know. These are the real forests—forests with charisma, forests that inspire, forests that can stimulate a sense of time immemorial.

We could not include every site, so our selection criteria became simple: we chose publicly accessible sites with a trail or clear route, and we included a range of the best and most impressive big-tree old-growth sites. We also selected a small number of charismatic dwarf old-growth sites, as well as examples of small groves, secondary old growth, and ecologically disturbed groves that are scenically impressive and/or historically significant.

Because most of the surviving eastern old growth has been discovered only in recent decades, the inventory process is new. Although ancient forests are among the most admired natural places to visit, there has never been a guidebook for people who wish to experience the inspiring groves of the Northeast. We are pleased that this is the first.

We hope this book will enhance your appreciation of ancient forests. The trees that live in old-growth forests are the oldest, tallest, and largest living life-forms on earth—worthy attributes in their own right. But ancient forests also offer a number of values that often go unrecognized. They are the living monuments that preserve the last surviving landscapes of the pre-European Native American landscape. They are the preferred habitats for numerous wildlife, including a high proportion of rare and endangered species. Serving as irreplaceable genetic banks, they preserve life-forms that achieve the greatest longevity, size, and survivability. They are scientific and educational resources, providing pristine outdoor laboratories. They also boost the economy as an ecotourist attraction, as the Redwoods and Great Smokies national parks and Cook Forest State Park attest.

Our goal is to share with you the noble forests of our land in the hope that your visits will enchant, excite, and create lasting memories of our eastern giants and other venerable trees. They are examples of nature's majesty, and their hushed green cathedrals are places of inspiration. May the ancient forests inspire you as they have inspired us.

Acknowledgments

Thanks to Jani Leverett for her unwavering support and to Helene Kershner for her love and patience in this long process. Thank you to those who assisted in the fieldwork: Jim Battaglia, Michael Siuta, Chuck Rosenburg, Glen Gelinas, Jerry Horowitz, Chris Walbrecht, Tom Diggins, Albert Garofalo, Western New York Old Growth Forest Survey Team; Fred Breglia; Tom Howard; Rob Henry; Dean Fitzgerald; Dan Karpen; Mark Dill; Ned Barnard; Bill Sweeney, Jamesburg State Park; David Burg; Bill Cain; Dale Luthringer; Will Stoner; Mike Demunn; Michael Kudish; Marcia and David Bonta; Matt Largess; Jud Newborn; Dave Kunstler, New York City Parks and Recreation; Tom Wessels; Dr. Edward Cook and Dr. Neil Pederson, Lamont Doherty Earth Observatory; Dr. Charles Canham; Chris Kane; Dr. Lee Carboneau; William Leak; Robert Van Pelt; Edward Frost; Jack Sobon; Lauren Stevens, Williams College; Paul Jost; Dr. Marc Abrams; Dr. Peter Dunwiddie; Dr. Lee Frelich;

Gary Beluzo; Dr. William Martin; Will Blozan; and Dr. David Orwig. We appreciate the help from those who provided information or other contributions: Mary Byrd Davis; Barbara McMartin; Robert Borg, Garth Woods Conservancy; Stephen Finn, National Park Service; Kyle Stockwell, Nature Conservancy, Maine Chapter; Eastern New York Chapter of the Nature Conservancy; Pat Cullina, Rutgers Gardens; Gary Salmon, Michael Fraysier, and Diana Frederick, Vermont Agency of Natural Resources; Bob Goodman, Wawayanda State Park, New Jersey; Bob Masson, Morristown National Historic Park, New Jersey; Dave Robertson, Pennypack Watershed Restoration Trust; John Symonds, Lancaster County Conservancy; Dale Prinkey, Jamesburg State Park; Robert Beleski, Pennsylvania Department of Conservation and Natural Resources; Nick Vaczek; Carol Woodin; Jeff McMullen; Dick Buegler and Protectors of Pine Oak Woods, Town of Vernon, Vermont; the staff at Dartmouth College Library; and Jeff Fullmer and Citizens Campaign for the Environment. Lastly, our gratitude goes to those who gave us their hospitality: Pearl Kershner, Randy and Amy Kaplan, Lois Lerman, Les Deines, and Sylvia Breitberg.

This is the forest primeval. The murmuring pines and the hemlocks,
Bearded with moss, and in garments green, indistinct in the twilight,
Stand like Druids of eld, with voices sad and prophetic. . .

—HENRY WADSWORTH LONGFELLOW, *EVANGELINE*

Introduction

Hushed, moss-hung forests; green cathedrals; majestic green patriarchs from which come the wisdom of the ancients; Druid temples of great oaks; towering sentinel pines; virgin forests"

These are some of the phrases that come to mind when people envision the great ancient forests encountered by the early European settlers on their arrival in North America. Writers boasted that the American forest was so extensive that a squirrel could travel from the Atlantic coast to the Mississippi from treetop to treetop, without ever touching the ground.

Sadly, it's all gone, they say.

Or is it?

As it turns out, despite the relentless plundering of the original forest, a few remnants still survive. Some areas of old growth are so extensive, in fact, they look like the original landscapes that never met with axe or chainsaw, bulldozer or plow—most notably in New York's Adirondacks, the South's

Great Smokies, Michigan's Porcupine Mountains, and Minnesota's Boundary Waters.

Throughout the Northeast, tracts of old-growth forest lie hidden in deep ravines, on cliffs, and on mountaintops. But many others flourish in accessible sites such as public parks and old family estates that are now nature preserves. All told, more than 400,000 acres of ancient forests still survive in the nine states of the Northeast.

A Brief History of Eastern Old Growth

The great virgin forests of eastern North America once covered as much as 950 million acres, but the early colonists from Europe had a decidedly negative impression of the forest. They described it as the "howling wilderness," a place that threatened their survival. It was dark and foreboding. It harbored wild animals—and Indians.

This perspective resulted in the first wave of forest destruction. Beginning in the 1600s, the settlers cleared land along the gentle slopes of the Atlantic coast for farms. By the 1700s, industrial exploiters moved into steeper, rockier, and more remote lands, cutting trees for lumber, tanbark, charcoal, and paper. When there were no more trees to cut, they set the land ablaze, sending raging fires across hundreds of thousands of acres in the Adirondacks and the mountains of New England. These bald summits are still visible to this day. In a mere 200 years, settlers and loggers had destroyed the vast virgin tracts of forest that had survived since the last Ice Age. Yet isolated parcels of old growth managed to escape destruction.

How Old Growth Survived

Beginning in the 1980s, a number of old-growth sleuths began discovering and documenting the existence of surviving forests. Although many of these stands are still being cut down, we believe roughly 2 million acres survived in the eastern United States—less than 0.5 percent of the original forest. The total for the Northeast is roughly 400,000 acres—only 0.64 percent of its original forest. With centuries of systematic logging and clearing, how were these precious parcels spared?

Old Public Properties By far, the most likely places to find surviving ancient forests are on lands that were put into public ownership between the 1800s and World War II, before logging reached them. These include national, state, and city park lands, national forests, and university and other institutional properties. The best-known example is the world-class 4,000-square-mile Adirondack State Forest Preserve, which contains 69 percent of the Northeast's surviving old-growth acreage. Other examples include Pennsylvania's Alan Seeger Natural Area, the Catskill State Forest Preserve, Allegany State Park in New York, and the New York Botanical Gardens.

Old Estates and Vacation Properties Many owners of large estates chose to leave part of their forest uncut. Some of these properties, which date back to the eighteenth century, are owned by descendants of original settlers who have retained the land without a break in continuity. Other properties were acquired by wealthy individuals to serve as their vacation resorts or secluded estates or by institutions to serve as camps and summer cottage sites. These sites often include lakefront groves of towering pines. In recent decades, some estate owners have donated or sold their properties to be used as parks or nature preserves. Massachusetts's William Cullen Bryant Preserve is an example. Other property owners, however, still choose to sell the land to a logging company or developer. In some lucky cases, the government or a nonprofit organization, such as the Nature Conservancy or Trust for Public Land, steps in to purchase and preserve these lands. A spectacular example is Minnewaska State Park in southern New York.

Inaccessible Lands or Poor Habitats for Timber Some ancient forest stands were protected due to remote or rugged locations that made them inaccessible to cutting. These places include steep ravine slopes and canyon bottoms, such as New York's Zoar Valley; the upper slopes and summits of the highest hills and mountains, including the Catskills; cliff edges and faces, such as the Delaware Water Gap in New Jersey; and extensive swamps and bogs like New Jersey's Bear Swamp.

Stands of Rural Land Owners Who Chose Forest Protection Very rarely, early farmers, settlers, or other rural landowners intentionally set aside the most inspiring or beautiful part of their forest holdings. These groves still inspire people in places like Pennsylvania's Cook Forest and Maine's Ordway Pines preserve.

Disputed Overlapping Properties This peculiar type of property occurs in remote lands where boundaries were unclear or overlapping. There were stiff penalties for cutting timber on someone else's land, so logging companies typically avoided these property corners. Dutlinger Natural Area in Pennsylvania and several sites in the Adirondacks are examples.

Defining "Old Growth"

Defining old-growth forests in the eastern United States is more complicated than it is in the west, where the antiquity of trees in these colossal forests is undisputed because of their great size. The genetic limits of eastern trees do not allow them to attain as great an age or stature. For eastern forests, we must ask: How old does a tree have to be for it to be considered "old" or "ancient"? Does a birch reach old age at the same time as a bald cypress? Is "ancient" for an individual tree the same as "ancient" for an entire forest made up of many different kinds of trees?

Another relevant question in defining old growth concerns the degree of human disturbance. Most old-growth forests have a history of very minor to modest human disturbance, involving selective logging, firewood cutting, maple sugaring, or grazing. Such forests are not pristine, but minor disturbance does not mean they can't be considered old growth. Some scientists and government officials assert that small old-growth groves—fewer than 20 acres and as small as 1 or 2 acres—do not qualify, either. But "old growth" refers to age. If most of the canopy trees in a forest are ancient—regardless of minor disturbance or size of stand—then the grove is ancient.

In this book, we present a basic definition of old-growth forest that is deliberately generic in order to cover the dazzling diversity of forest types: old-growth (or ancient) forest has a canopy dominated by trees at least 150 years old. The age of 150 years is based on the collective experience of many old-growth researchers who have found it is a relatively consistent age at which bark, trunk, and forest structure develop clearly observable features (see pages 33–36) that contrast markedly with younger trees and forests. These features develop due to repeated exposure to severe weather and a long duration of growth and succession.

CATEGORIES OF OLD GROWTH

Within the broad array of old-growth forests we describe in this book, there are four categories, which apply generally to eastern U.S. temperate-zone forests.

Primary Old Growth This kind of old-growth forest is a natural community with a canopy dominated by trees 150 years or older that has been continuously forested since before European settlement. Related names are presettlement, primeval, original, and first-growth forest. All sites in this book are primary old growth unless otherwise stated.

Virgin Old Growth These are primary old-growth forests that have had no intentional disturbance by humans (although they may have had unintentional disturbances from climatic effects, such as acid rain, or wildlife, such as deer overbrowsing). While these are the rarest of all old growth, virgin forests still cover thousands of acres in the Adirondacks. Other sizable virgin forests include Maine's Big Reed Pond Preserve, some mountain slopes of New Hampshire's White Mountains, parts of New York's Green Lakes State Park and Zoar Valley, and, of course, Pennsylvania's Cook Forest.

In the past, many people considered old growth and virgin to be synonymous, so for them, sites with any human disturbance could not be called old growth. Even today, some scientists, agency officials, and foresters maintain this unrealistically rigid position—which would rule out nearly every site in this book.

Secondary Old Growth This type of forest originated after European settlement but has a canopy dominated by trees 150 years or older. Although it was logged or cleared in the 1600s to early 1800s, it was left to naturally reforest, developing canopy trees that range from 150 to 300 years old. Because secondary old growth does not consist of original forest, some people debate whether it meets the definition of old growth.

While secondary old-growth forests have less scientific significance than primary old growth, their trees can attain as great a size and height as original old-growth forests. Their aesthetic, historic, and cultural value is often as great as that of the original forests. Connecticut's secondary old-growth Cathedral Pines, for instance, were cited as the finest old-growth stand in all of New England before a 1989 storm blew much of it down. Perhaps the best-known stand of secondary old growth is England's Sherwood Forest. It was completely cut long ago, then allowed to reforest in a protected sanctuary. Today, 900 of its trees are 600 or more years old!

Urban Old Growth Mostly found in old city parks and on former wealthy estates, urban old-growth forests have trees that range from 250 to 450 years of age and typically live in forest groves of small acreage. These sites are valuable, nonetheless, because they are accessible to the greatest number of people—including those in New York City, who can visit a 25-acre stand on Manhattan.

Because of their proximity to urban stresses, however, these forests cannot be judged by the same standards as more wild ancient forests. They are likely to have many kinds of disturbance, from invasion by exotic plant species to litter and vandalism or erosion from street runoff.

GROWTH FORMS OF OLD-GROWTH TREES

As a whole, old-growth trees appear in three different forms: big-tree, dwarf, and medium stature. Big-tree forests, the primary type in this book, comprise the classic large-diameter trees. The most common northeastern big-tree species are oaks, sugar and red maples, eastern hemlock, eastern white pine, white ash, yellow birch, American beech, American basswood, American sycamore, and black cherry.

Dwarf old-growth trees appear as bonsai, twisted, gnarled, and even upside-down shapes. These trees—most commonly red and northern white cedar, hemlock, yellow and black birch, pitch pine, red spruce, black gum, American holly, and northern red and chestnut oaks—grow in severe habitats, such as cliffs, steep rocky slopes, summits, sand dunes, barrens, and bogs. Though small in size, the cliff cedars and pitch pines inexplicably grow much older than they do on healthy growing sites, with the white cedars reaching the greatest ages of all northeastern trees—up to 1,700 years.

Medium-stature old growth is neither impressive in size nor charismatic in character. It therefore must be recognized by other features, such as the ones described in the following pages.

FEATURES OF AN OLD-GROWTH FOREST

The primary feature of an old-growth forest is a large proportion of ancient trees. A scientist can measure the exact age of individual trees by counting their annual rings, but fortunately ancient forests display external features that also indicate old growth.

Use a tree identification guide to note the kinds of trees in each of the ancient forests you visit. In big-tree forests, the most common species are those known to be long-lived, such as hemlock; cedar; white, red, black, bur, and chestnut oak; sugar and red maple; tulip tree; white and red pine; red spruce; yellow and black birch; white ash; black cherry; beech; shagbark hickory; sycamore; and black gum.

Experts searching for old growth consider it an especially good sign to find large specimens of commercially prized species, such as black cherry, black walnut, white pine, and cedar. This tells them the area has not been logged for a century or more. They also look for signs of extensive logging or human disturbance that would rule out old growth. These signs include stumps, stone walls, old logging roads, trees with low and wide spreading boughs, tree plantations, or trees associated with younger forests, such as aspen, poplar, willow, black locust, hawthorn, or white birch.

When you visit, you can look for the following physical features of the trees that indicate old growth.

Large Trunks Trunks that are 30 inches or greater in diameter are the most easily recognizable indicators of old growth. The large trunk rule cannot be used alone, however. It does-not apply to fast-growing species such as poplar, aspen, cottonwood, and willow. Species such as hemlock, cedar, black gum, and yellow and black birch can grow very slowly and become ancient with diameters of only 5 to 15 inches. Trees growing under very healthy growing conditions—especially red oak, red maple, and tulip tree—can sometimes grow rather large before reaching 150 years in age.

Antique Bark This may be the most reliable feature. When trees reach ages of around 150 years, the bark of most species frequently develops balding, deep furrowing, shagginess, or large separate plates. The higher up the trunk this bark appears, the more ancient the tree is likely to be.

Buttressed Roots These trees display large trunk bases that flare out or swell with prominent root projections.

Tall, Branchless Trunks These include classic towering trunks whose lowest boughs start at 25 to 40 feet or more up the trunk. First boughs have been recorded as high up as 120 feet. These indicate the tree grew in a deeply shaded forest for a long time before reaching the canopy.

"Stag-Headed" Tree Tops Ancient tree crowns, especially in oaks, maples, tulip trees, and pines, can take shapes suggesting antlers, with thick boughs projecting out at right angles, topped by contorted branches. Repeated battering by ice storms and wind breakage causes this.

Bizarre Growth Forms Among the most unique aspects of ancient forests are the picturesque shapes trees develop over many centuries. Look for some of the following on your next visit to an old forest:

- knotty, knobby, burly, misshapen, and charismatic trunks; some primeval trees have giant, round burls up to 6 feet wide on their massive trunks

- "stilt-roots" (hemlock, yellow birch, red maple) that support the trunk several feet (to as high as 10 feet) off the forest floor

- "bonsai" or "daredevil" trees (hemlocks, cedars, birches, pines) that project their trunks horizontally out from cliffs

- spiral-grain trunks (maples, cherries) that display a conspicuous twist or grain; these are possibly formed as a survival response by canopy trees to the torque caused by buffeting winds, to prevent breakage or toppling

- zigzag-shaped trunks, "lover" trees (fused trunks of different species), window trees (formed by fused boughs), and upside-down trees, such as the northern white cedars growing on limestone cliffs

Numerous Large Logs Logged forests really mean "de-logged" forests—that is, the large trunks are removed. Large amounts of logs, snags (standing dead trees), and accumulations of old branches and decaying leaves (called "coarse woody debris") are common in many ancient forests.

Pit and Mound Undulations on the Forest Floor This phenomenon develops when, over a period of centuries, many big trees are blown over. Roots rip out, leaving a shallow pit, while the root mass and large trunk gradually decay back into soil, leaving a 2- to 3-foot mound as a subtle monument to the former tree.

Rich Growth of Moss, Fungi, and Lichens Because it takes centuries of undisturbed conditions for moss to grow upward from a tree base, moss is an especially good sign of age if it is growing 6 or more feet up a trunk. (This is not applicable to upper mountain forests where cloud fog accelerates moss growth.) Moss is most likely to grow up trunks of yellow birch, ash, and sugar maple. Great length of time also allows old-growth forests to develop thick organic soils rich in dense moss beds, ferns, lichens, and liverworts, as well as abundant and diverse populations of mushrooms and other fungi. Dozens of lichen, moss, and fungi species grow nowhere else except in ancient forests.

How to Appreciate Ancient Trees

Although the old forests of the eastern United States will never measure up to the size of the famed redwoods and sequoias of the west, eastern trees have their own distinctive features that any visitor can enjoy. Some of these trees have been around for 500 years (and a few for 2,000), which has allowed them to develop character beyond size and stature.

On your visit to eastern forests, expect the tallest trees to stand at 115 to 150 feet, unless you visit the Great Smoky Mountains, South Carolina's Congaree Swamp, or Pennsylvania's Cook Forest, where some grow upwards of 165 to 200 feet. Champion trees—those that are the tallest or largest in their species—may have diameters between 6 and

15 feet thick. But you should expect most large trees to be 3 to 5 feet in diameter.

To truly appreciate the size of ancient and champion trees in the Northeast, always follow these rules—and don't be shy about getting close to the trees!

- Walk right up to a tree's trunk and put your hand on it. Look up. This gives you a human scale to understand the greatness of the tree.

- Gauge a great tree's true size by how many arm spreads it takes to go around the trunk. (Besides, after centuries of enduring hurricanes, windstorms, lightning, disease, droughts, and vandalism, wouldn't you want a hug, too?)

- Note how high a tree soars before reaching its first thick bough (for towering trees). Observe whether the boughs form a stag-headed shape.

- Appreciate peculiar personality features, such as buttressed roots (bulging trunk base), giant knots and burls, lightning scars, carpets of moss on the trunk, spiral twisted trunk, deep furrows, peeling plates on the bark, or balding bark. These indicate great age or are examples of the charismatic features seen only in ancient trees.

- Spread the word about these primeval treasures. This book features 134 old-growth sites, less than a third of the known sites—but there are bound to be more. Who knows, you could be the one to discover the "newest" ancient forest.

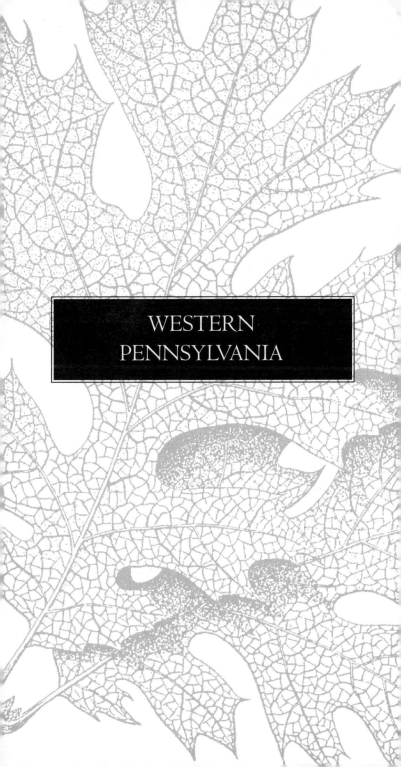

WESTERN
PENNSYLVANIA

Pennsylvania's primeval forests are legendary. Its floodplain sycamores, black walnut trees, and American chestnuts were colossal, with one chestnut reaching an astounding 17 feet in diameter. Six million acres of the Allegheny plateau's Black Forest formed the epicenter of the country's eastern hemlock forest. Penn's Woods, as the state was once called, led the nation in lumber production after New York's Adirondack Mountains lost that distinction around 1860.

Today, the virgin big-tree remnants of this once-great forest province add up to between 8,000 and 10,000 acres, but some of the trees that were growing when William Penn took possession of this land in 1681 are still standing tall. This is in large part because Pennsylvania began setting aside old-growth forests in public preserves in 1909; it was just one of two eastern states to do so. At that time, state land managers were asked to nominate for preservation their favorite virgin forests that survived the logging boom. A 1921 law establishing the first old-growth inventory was soon followed by state initiatives that have given Pennsylvania the most extensive and well-organized system of protected ancient forests of any eastern state.

Today, Pennsylvania has fifty-two big-tree old-growth sites comprising 0.06 percent of Pennsylvania's forest area. Twenty-four of those sites are in state parks or natural areas. Of thirty-eight publicly owned sites, six are in federal lands, primarily Allegheny National Forest and Delaware Water Gap National Recreation Area; eight sites are in private non-profit or similar preserves; and six are in unprotected, private ownership. We suspect there are more old-growth sites on public and private lands, but no systematic search is currently under way.

Pennsylvania also possesses up to 20,000 acres of woodland that was never logged because it had no commercial value: small-stature, open woodlands of pitch pine and scrub oak on dry ridge tops, barrens, and other poor sites. These trees are genetically short-lived or live in fire- and windstorm-prone communities.

Western Pennsylvania is home to some of the largest, highest-quality, and best-known examples of virgin old-growth forest. This is surprising, since this region is also where the rapacious logging industry once thrived. Cook Forest, the Tionesta Natural Area, Heart's Content, and the Alan Seeger Natural Area are four such examples. Cook Forest's 1,500-acre old growth boasts the Northeast's tallest forest and one of the world's tallest eastern white pines. The 3,200-acre forest at Tionesta is the Northeast's second largest ancient forest outside the Adirondacks. The 120-acre forest in the Alan Seeger Natural Area is one of the oldest forests in the Northeast. The stand at Heart's Content, in the Allegheny National Forest, was one of the first to be protected in the Northeast and one of the two most widely known ancient forests in eastern North America.

Like these stands, the majority of western Pennsylvania's known ancient forests are on public lands that were set aside during the early-twentieth-century state initiatives. Although a few more sites in newer state parks and non-profit preserves have been protected since that time, there have been no systematic old-growth surveys in western Pennsylvania, and we believe a ten-year survey would probably turn up fifty or more ancient forests in the state's western half alone.

I. COOK FOREST STATE PARK

The gem of the Northeast's old-growth woodlands is Cook Forest State Park. In this forest cathedral, nature has made a grand statement with 1,500 acres of inspiring old growth. Cook Forest itself features 27 miles of trails winding through 8,000 acres.

Though the ages of the trees (250 to 400 years) and their trunk sizes (up to 48 inches in diameter) are impressive, it is their vertical dimension that is truly exceptional. In this forest—the Northeast's tallest—lofty patriarchs of white pine rise majestically through a lower canopy of craggy hemlocks and shaggy hardwoods that are champions in their own right.

Cook Forest excels in superlatives, as it boasts the single tallest, accurately measured tree in the Northeast, the Longfellow Pine, which towers 180.9 feet, as well as the Seneca Pine, which, at 172 feet tall and 48 inches in diameter, may be Pennsylvania's largest white pine in volume (almost 1,000 cubic feet). The park is also home to more than sixty other pines more than 150 feet tall, including two others taller than 170 feet. The hemlocks here are showpieces, too, with heights exceeding 125 feet and diameters of up to 40 inches.

But Cook Forest is not just tall pines. The hardwoods— including northern red oak, American beech, black cherry, red maple, and white ash—also soar. The average height of the ten tallest species in Cook Forest is 134.05 feet, the highest average in the Northeast.

The hushed splendor of Cook Forest made it a popular destination as far back as the nineteenth century. In 1927, citizens rallied with the first U.S. Forest Service director, Gifford Pinchot, to save these trees. In 1928, Anthony W. Cook donated it to the state as one of the country's first parks established solely to save an ancient forest.

■ DIRECTIONS

Take I-80 to Exit 78. Take Route 36 north to Cooksburg and Cook Forest State Park. You can see the big trees from your car by driving the old one-way fire road off Route 36, leading to the Seneca Tower.

■ HIGHLIGHTS

Most people marvel at the great matriarchs along the trails of the Forest Cathedral Area. Pick up a trail map at the Log Cabin Visitor Center.

Most of the champion-size trees, including the Longfellow Pine, grow along the Longfellow Trail, a 1.2-mile loop that starts behind the visitor center. Use your map to stay on the main trail, since a maze of small trails branches off from it.

One of the most visually striking routes is the Hemlock

Trail, a continuation of the Longfellow Trail. As its name suggests, it features towering hemlocks, with a fern understory reminiscent of the Pacific Northwest. This trail joins the park road with Route 36.

The Seneca Trail begins where Route 36 crosses the Clarion River. Here the forest has an intriguing primeval look. The park's tallest hemlocks, some reaching as high as 142 feet, share the grove with enormous pines. As the trail climbs to the impressive overlook at Seneca Tower, it enters a drier forest with smaller, but equally old, trees.

Ancient broadleaf hardwoods, such as oak, maple, cherry, and ash, surround Indian Trail, Joyce Kilmer Trail, and Rhododendron Trail. Baker Trail, in the northwest section of the park, features a primeval wetland with large and very old hemlocks.

■ **CONTACT INFORMATION**

Cook Forest State Park, P.O. Box 120, Cooksburg, Pennsylvania 16217, 814-744-8407

2. HEART'S CONTENT

Heart's Content, located in Allegheny National Forest, is the most well known and best-studied old-growth forest in the Northeast. This 150-acre grove boasts striking specimens of white pine and hemlock ranging in age from 300 to 400 years. It is also Pennsylvania's second tallest forest, with one white pine reaching 163.3 feet, and eleven others more than 150 feet. Locals have sold T-shirts boasting, "Heart's Content, Where Virgins Still Stand Tall." Diameters of 36 to 54 inches are typical of the trees here.

The largest white pine in volume is 49 inches thick and 157.6 feet tall. Other impressive elders include American beech, sugar maple, red maple, and black cherry. One black cherry is 118 feet in height—notable for this species. The average height of the ten tallest species is a respectable 113.79 feet.

In 1923, *American Forestry* described the white pines growing here as "some of the finest specimens of this world-famous forest tree." A single quarter-acre section of the Heart's Content stand was estimated to contain 50,000 board feet of lumber. The largest pine at that time measured 52 inches in diameter.

Unfortunately, the future of this treasure is threatened. Ozone and acid rain pollution, together with beech blight and deer overbrowsing, are killing many of the trees, and the cathedral canopy is now open in places.

■ **DIRECTIONS**

From Route 6 in Warren, Pennsylvania, take Route 337 south for 11 miles to a dirt road on the left. Follow the signs to Heart's Content.

■ **HIGHLIGHTS**

The easy nature trail starts from the parking lot. Once you are inside the forest, take the longer, 1-mile trail loop. Wandering off the trail will take you into parts of the grove that retain a more cathedral-like feeling.

■ **CONTACT INFORMATION**

Allegheny National Forest, 222 Liberty Street, P.O. Box 847, Warren, Pennsylvania 16365, 814-723-5150

3. ANDERS RUN

Lordly giants soar above you, while the murmur of the brook fills the ravine below you at the 50-acre Anders Run Natural Area. If you are here when it is windy, you will be treated to the mystical whoosh of millions of pine needles combing the breeze.

One colossal, 300-year-old white pine, 54 inches in diameter and 163 feet in height, rises above the trail, and at least two other pines reach 150 feet. The ten tallest species average 118.65 feet.

Although state forest officials claim this is a second-growth site, logged in the early 1800s, our annual ring counts show this site is mostly original forest. We have found 400-year-old hemlocks, 20 to 45 inches in diameter, and 300-year-old pines in the old-growth acreage of the ravine. Other old-growth trees in this forest are red and white oak, sugar and red maple, black and yellow birch, and the uncommon cucumber magnolia.

■ **DIRECTIONS**

Take Interstate 86/17 in New York State to the exit for Route 62 south. Drive 28 miles to Warren, Pennsylvania. Route 62 joins with Route 6. Drive 5.7 miles on Route 62/6 and exit the highway to follow Route 62 south. After a half mile, turn right at a sign for the Buckaloons Recreation Area, just before the bridge over Allegheny River. Drive 0.7 mile and turn left on Dunns Eddy Road. Drive 0.9 mile to a pull-off on the left with the sign for Cornplanter State Forest—Anders Run. Pick up a map in the wooden box, but don't park here. Continue ahead, making the first right onto Allegheny Springs Road. In three-quarters of a mile, park at the third pull-off on your left.

■ **HIGHLIGHTS**

Walk across the footbridge over Anders Run brook. The yellow trail climbs steadily through magnificent old growth to the top of the ravine. After a quarter mile, look carefully to your left for the largest pine, 150 feet off the trail at the edge of the ravine. The trail soon descends and crosses another footbridge. Turn right after the bridge and follow the trail as it winds around to Dunns Mill Road.

Look across the road here for the Little Stone House in the Hollow, built in 1841. Then head north, watching for the trail blaze on the right, where you will head back into the woods. At the next parking lot, cross Dunns Mill Road. Bear left at any forks in the trail. The trail curves to your left and returns to your car.

■ **CONTACT INFORMATION**

Cornplanter State Forest District, 323 North State Street, North Warren, Pennsylvania 16365, 814-723-0262

4. Tionesta Natural Area

It took a millennium to create these primeval woods within the Allegheny National Forest Natural Area, but it took only minutes for a 1985 tornado to obliterate nearly a quarter of its acreage. Fortunately, the storm missed roughly 3,200 acres, and Tionesta remains Pennsylvania's most extensive old-growth forest. In the silence of this grove today, there is no hint of the violence that once ravaged the area.

Today, sentinel hemlocks 4 feet thick and up to 600 years old tower above centuries-old sugar maple, beech, and yellow birch. Huge black cherry trees grow among large tulip trees, red maple, basswood, black birch, white pine, white ash, and even cucumber magnolia. Unfortunately, a storm in the fall of 2003 blew down many trees around the trail.

■ DIRECTIONS

Take I-80 in Pennsylvania to Exit 16 and drive north 48 miles on Route 219. Turn west on Route 6. When Route 6 meets Route 66 in Kane Village, set your odometer. Drive exactly 9 miles to Ludlow. Watch for a sign to Tionesta Scenic Area, and turn left onto South Hillside Street. A second sign directs you to turn left onto Water Street. Soon after that, you'll see a third sign saying 6.6 miles to Tionesta. Turn right on Scenic Road and immediately cross railroad tracks. National Forest Road 133 begins here. Set your odometer. Bear left at the next fork and follow Road 133 for exactly 5.5 miles. Drive to the far end of the road's dead-end loop and park where you see the sign for the trail.

■ HIGHLIGHTS

The Nature Trail takes you through only a small portion of the ancient forest. Start off under large hemlocks and bear left at the fork to stay on the longer loop. In a half mile, the trail reaches a cleared corridor for a pipeline right-of-way. Turn left. Walk to the edge of the valley view to see the site of the 1985 tornado. The tornado left untouched old growth on ridges along both margins. An impenetrable thicket of aspen, beech, and hop hornbeam is now growing in the tornado zone. In 25 more years, a young forest will be established. In 200 more years, ancient forest will return.

Return along the pipeline corridor but pass the trail that you came in on. Walk several hundred more feet, watching for a white arrow pointing to the right, where you reenter the forest. At a fork with white arrows (the short loop), take the left fork to return.

- **CONTACT INFORMATION**

Allegheny National Forest, 222 Liberty Street, P.O. Box 847, Warren, Pennsylvania 16365, 814-723-5150

5. FERNCLIFF IN OHIOPYLE STATE PARK

Ohiopyle State Park is the Northeast's white-water rafting capital and, at 19,052 acres, Pennsylvania's second largest park. Most of the 2 million people who visit the thundering Ohiopyle Falls have no idea that a 15-acre old-growth forest lines the opposite shore. Ancient hemlock, black birch, tulip tree, oaks, and rhododendron vegetate Ferncilff Peninsula's ledges along the raging river for 1.5 miles.

- **DIRECTIONS**

Take Pennsylvania Turnpike (Route 76) to Exit 9. Go two miles south on Route 711. Join Route 381 south and take it all the way to the Ohiopyle park entrance.

- **HIGHLIGHTS**

At the visitor center in a historic train station, pick up a Ferncliff map, then drive back across the river and immediately turn left to the trail parking area.

At the river end of the lot, head downstream on the 1.8-

mile trail, taking the shore trail (the outside loop). Visit each river vista. Follow the trail around the peninsula, always taking the path forks that veer toward the river.

■ **CONTACT INFORMATION**

Ohiopyle State Park, P.O. Box 105, Ohiopyle, Pennsylvania 15470, 724-329-5891

6. LAUREL HILL STATE PARK

The closest known old-growth site to Pittsburgh is a 7-acre remnant of ancient hemlocks along the south side of the creek in Laurel Hill State Park. The trees here range between 200 and 300 years of age and have diameters of up to 42 inches. Their aged bark is ruddy and corrugated. Wood sorrel and wood fern adorn the forest floor.

■ **DIRECTIONS**

Take Route 76 to Exit 10. Go south on Route 601 into Somerset. Turn right (west) and drive 7.2 miles on Route 31. Turn left at the sign for Laurel Hill State Park. Drive 1.6 miles on Route 3037. Turn right on the park road at the stone entrance gates. Go 0.4 mile to the park office and pick up a map. Drive 0.5 mile more and park in the gravel lot on the right just before the bridge over the creek.

■ **HIGHLIGHTS**

Walk across the bridge and follow the sign on the right to the 1.2-mile Hemlock Trail. In 0.2 mile, turn left on the blue-blazed trail. Head up the hill. After passing ruins of a lean-to, you reach grand hemlocks. At the next trail junction, take the left trail (blue). At one more trail junction, turn right on the yellow trail. The largest hemlock is at the next trail intersection. Stay left and follow the yellow trail back.

■ **CONTACT INFORMATION**
Laurel Hill State Park, R.D. 4, Box 130, Somerset, Pennsylvania 15501, 814-445-7725

7. SWEET ROOT NATURAL AREA

Upon entering the Sweet Root Natural Area, you'll feel like you're the first human to set foot in this remote virgin forest. About 69 acres of primeval hemlock, oak, black birch, basswood, and white pine fill the rugged hidden notch carved by Sweet Root Creek's tributary. Toppled trees and logs lie across jumbles of mossy boulders.

In 1902, the state of Pennsylvania purchased Sweet Root ravine, which now lies within a 1,403-acre natural area in Buchanan State Forest, only 8 miles from the Maryland border. In 1921, it was recommended as one of the original nine Pennsylvania state forest monuments, recognized for its old-growth value. Unfortunately, woolly adelgid insect pests are now killing the hemlocks.

■ **DIRECTIONS**
Take Route 76 (Pennsylvania Turnpike) to Exit 11, and head south on Route 220 into Bedford. Turn left (east) on Route 30, then turn right (south) on Route 326. Set your odometer. Drive 13.8 miles on Route 326, watching on your

right for Sweet Root Road to the picnic area. If you pass Black Valley Road or Chaneysville, you've gone too far.

■ **HIGHLIGHTS**

Head west into the woods on the road behind the gate. Pass small fields and ignore any trail that does not stay on the south side of the stream corridor. In a mile, the trail ends at a dark hemlock forest in a notch. Bushwhack along the stream through virgin forest. After 0.75 mile, the stream turns north and the valley opens up. Follow the stream until the old growth ends. Return the way you came.

■ **CONTACT INFORMATION**

Buchanan State Forest, 440 Buchanan Trail, McConnellsburg, Pennsylvania 17233, 717-485-3148

8. HEMLOCKS NATURAL AREA

The majestic matriarchs of the 131-acre Hemlocks Natural Area are the true royalty of the Tuscarora State Forest. With its abundance of giant hemlocks (Pennsylvania's state tree) and the timeless flow of a nearby brook, this is a place to be revered for eternity. Indeed, Congress designated this site a National Natural Landmark in 1973.

Here the shaggy hemlocks are 330 to 500 years old, up to 123 feet tall, and up to 54 inches in diameter. Ancient yellow birch, including many with buttressed roots, also thrive here, as do mountain laurel, which blossom pink in June. In some trees, pileated woodpeckers have sculpted trunks with deep and elongated holes.

Take I-76 (Pennsylvania Turnpike) to Exit 16. Take Route 11 into Carlisle and make a left (south) onto Route 34. In several blocks, turn right on Route 641, then right again on Route 74 north. In 14 miles, turn left on Route 850. After 3.8 miles, 850 joins Route 274, which you follow for 18.4 miles west. Turn south on Hemlock Road and go 4 miles to the parking lot.

■ **HIGHLIGHTS**

From the parking lot, take the wood chip-covered path downhill. Cross the wood bridge over the creek and turn right to explore upstream. At the stream crossing, return to the bridge and head downstream (not uphill into the woods) on the red trail. Cross the stream and continue, ignoring any left-hand trails. A half mile from the first bridge, cross another bridge on your right and turn right on the yellow trail. Take advantage of the benches along the trail to enjoy the timeless essence of the forest.

For a longer, 1.75-mile walk, take a left on the other side. Follow the yellow trail to the orange trail and continue straight ahead to Hemlock Road. Follow the orange trail to the yellow trail and take this all the way to the first bridge. Cross it and take the trail back to your car.

See more old growth at the nearby Frank Masland Natural Area. From the Hemlocks Natural Area parking lot, turn right and continue heading east on Hemlock Road. In about 5 miles, make the first right. In a half mile, continue straight on Union Hollow Road. In about 2 miles, turn right onto

Laurel Run Road, which winds for about 6 miles. Watch carefully on the left for the sign "Phoenix Bridge Access" on your right, just after a small bridge over Laurel Run and before the road curves sharply to the right. Turn into the hidden parking area with a large "Natural Area" sign on the left. Walk along the North Fork Trail for 1.2 miles downstream past sections of ancient forest. Return the way you came.

■ CONTACT INFORMATION
Tuscarora State Forest, P.O. Box 67, Blain, Pennsylvania 17006, 717-536-3191

9. ALAN SEEGER NATURAL AREA

Flat, easy paths weave through evergreen tunnels of rhododendron, pierced by enduring hemlocks, many 600 or more years old, 112 feet tall, and 50 inches thick, in the Alan Seeger Natural Area. This remarkable sanctuary is currently considered the oldest big-tree forest in the Northeast. Virgin tulip trees reach champion heights of 137.5 feet. Yellow birch, black gum, white pine, red maple, and northern red, white, and chestnut oak also grow in this ravine. The 120-acre Alan Seeger Natural Area is, according to famed botanist E. Lucy Braun, "a perfect example of a hemlock forest."

This treasure, named in 1921 for a World War I soldier and poet killed in France, is one of the first groves in the Northeast to be set aside specifically because it was virgin forest. How it survived is a mystery. Former logging roads come right up to the grove, and the entire surrounding area was clear-cut. There was even a sawmill and charcoal operation on one side and a logging railroad on the other.

■ DIRECTIONS

Take I-80 in Pennsylvania to Exit 24 and head south on Route 26. Before entering State College, take Route 322 for 17 miles to Laurel Creek Reservoir. The road steeply descends to the reservoir and then follows its shore. Just before a sharp bend to the left, look for Stone Creek Road on your right. Turn here, drive 0.1 mile, and turn right again. Drive west for 7.3 miles to the parking lot where Stone Creek Road and Seeger Road meet.

■ HIGHLIGHTS

Get a trail map at the large wooden sign before the parking area and start your walk here. In a quarter mile, pass the Greenwood Spur of the Mid-State Trail system and stay on the Seeger Loop Trail. You'll see the oldest trees on an island in Stone Creek. Here, we have counted 600 rings on the remains of a recently fallen hemlock.

When the trail curves around, turn right on Seeger Road. Cross Stone Creek and turn right on the Mill Race Trail, which takes you to a 500-year-old hemlock. This part of the stream was diverted to power a sawmill just downstream. Return to Seeger Road and your car.

■ CONTACT INFORMATION

Rothrock State Forest, P.O. Box 403, Rothrock Lane, Huntingdon, Pennsylvania 16652, 814-643-2340

10. DETWEILER RUN

Only 2.25 miles from Alan Seeger Natural Area, Detweiler Run has up to 185 acres of shaggy senior citizens. This enchanting forest of 300- to 400-year-old trees includes hemlock sages up to 54 inches thick, as well as virgin white pine, yellow birch, and a tangled understory of rhododendron and moss hummocks.

■ DIRECTIONS

From Alan Seeger Natural Area, drive west on Stone Creek Road. At 0.4 mile, turn right onto dirt Bear Meadows Road. At 1.7 miles, you come to a sharp turn. Park just before the turn, at the gated dirt road on the right.

■ HIGHLIGHTS

Walk down the gated woods road a half mile to a sign for Detweiler Natural Area. Walk a short distance farther and turn right. The orange trail skirts the ancient forest, bringing you tantalizingly close but not into the interior of the woods.

To go safely off-trail, look for a faint path on your left after a quarter of a mile (where the sound of the brook is loudest). Push past rhododendron for 10 feet to a clear area with a fire ring. If you wish, walk left and bushwhack along the stream a short way to sample more of this special place. When you return to the main trail, turn left. When you reach signs for the Mid-State Trail, turn right and head uphill to the gated road. Turn left to return.

■ CONTACT INFORMATION

Rothrock State Forest, P.O. Box 403, Rothrock Lane, Huntingdon, Pennsylvania 16652, 814-643-2340

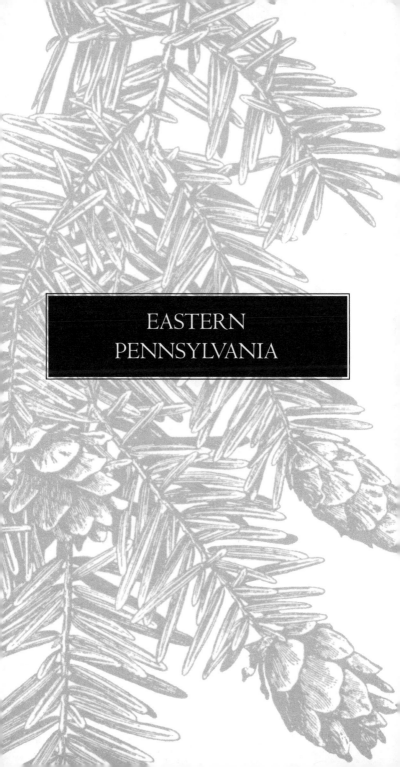

EASTERN
PENNSYLVANIA

In eastern Pennsylvania, waterfalls helped save the majority of the ancient forests that survive today. There are at least forty waterfalls in this region, and about 40 percent of the known old-growth forests here were not cut because they contributed to the scenic attraction of the falls. In the nineteenth-century Romantic Era, tourists flocked to local waterfalls as people today do to national parks. Newspaper reporters and philosophers praised their mystical beauty, which was also glorified in paintings, poems, and postcards. Because of this strong public sentiment and the profits from the fees tourists paid to see these waterfalls, estate owners chose to preserve the surrounding forests.

In the Northeast as a whole, 10 to 15 percent of old-growth forests include waterfalls. The most famous combination of falls and ancient forests in the Northeast is in eastern Pennsylvania's Ricketts Glen State Park, which has at least 2,000 acres of old growth surrounding twenty-two waterfalls. Other notable forests surrounding waterfalls include Delaware Water Gap National Recreation Area, with six cascades; the stands surrounding the gorges of the Susquehanna River, which has four falls; and Salt Springs State Park, with three cascades and 20 acres of old-growth forest.

Many of the other ancient forests in eastern Pennsylvania were spared because their locations in gorges were difficult to reach by old-fashioned logging methods. Most of the region's remaining sites survived because the landowners valued the trees' beauty over their financial worth, and some were set aside by the early-twentieth-century initiatives that preserved virgin forests on a statewide level. Four stands of ancient forests— including the Snyder-Middleswarth Natural Area, one of Pennsylvania's tallest forests, and the adjacent Tall Timbers Natural Area—were spared in this way.

Like parts of western Pennsylvania, the Philadelphia metro area has yet to be extensively surveyed for old-growth forests. There are only three known groves of ancient trees in this region, but we expect some lucky tree explorers will find more.

11. RICKETTS GLEN STATE PARK

At 13,134 acres, Ricketts Glen is Pennsylvania's largest state park, boasting a stair-stepping series of twenty-two waterfalls and 2,000 acres of magnificent primeval forest. The world record age for a hemlock, 988 years, was recorded here for a tree that fell decades ago. Little is known about the age of the hemlocks growing here today.

An inspiring 3.5-mile trail winds through the glen and its ten waterfalls. Although one falls stretches 94 feet, several trees are even higher, including a white ash of 127.2 feet, a tulip tree of 126.6 feet, and hemlocks as high as 118 feet. Tree diameters are 30 to 48 inches. You'll also find old-growth white pine, northern red and white oak, yellow birch, and sugar maple.

The glen was named after Colonel Robert Rickett, a Battle of Gettysburg hero who logged 80,000 acres of surrounding forest, but forbade lumbering the forest of his own estate, near the glen's falls.

■ DIRECTIONS

In Pennsylvania, take I-80 to Exit 35. Drive north on Route 487 to the park.

■ HIGHLIGHTS

Pick up a trail map at the park entrance and hike down Ganoga Glen Trail past ten waterfalls to Waters Meet intersection. Follow Kitchen Creek Trail downstream past three more waterfalls and more ancient forest. Backtrack to Waters Meet again and take Glen Leigh Trail upstream past more old growth and eight waterfalls. At the top of the ravine, take the first left onto Highland Trail. Pass through intriguing Midway Crevasse before reaching the trailhead.

To access the southern virgin forest, follow Route 118 until it crosses Kitchen Creek. Take the trail into Boston Run Natural Area and Adams Falls.

■ CONTACT INFORMATION

Ricketts Glen State Park, 695 State Route 487, Benton, Pennsylvania 17814, 570-477-5675

12. Snyder-Middleswarth Natural Area

Time stands still in the Snyder-Middleswarth Natural Area. In this solemn place, hallowed white pines soar above a sparkling clear brook in one of the Northeast's best primeval forests.

It is easy to feel poetic here, where you will find Pennsylvania's tallest hemlock towering at 142.8 feet. Some of the hemlocks grow up to 48 inches in diameter, and they range in age from 250 to 500 years. Ancient yellow and black birches and red maples grow here, too, surrounded by lush carpets of moss covering rocks, logs, and trees along the brook.

The state purchased this tract in 1902, later recognizing it as a State Natural Area. Congress designated it a National Natural Landmark in the 1960s. While Snyder-Middleswarth is virgin, adjoining Tall Timbers Natural Area has had selective cutting, making it a mix of original and second growth. Together, these two natural areas cover 600 acres of Bald Eagle State Forest.

■ **DIRECTIONS**

Take I-80 in Pennsylvania to Exit 30. Take Route 15 south for 6.8 miles. In Lewisburg, turn right (west) on Route 45 and drive 17.5 miles. Turn left on Route 235 and drive 9.2 miles. Entering Troxelville, look for a large sign for Snyder-Middleswarth Picnic Area and Tall Timbers. Turn right here and follow Swift Run Road for 4.7 miles. Follow the sign for Tall Timbers past Rock Springs Picnic Area and turn right into Snyder-Middleswarth Picnic Area.

Begin walking on the trail to the left of the sign for Tall Timbers Trail and the bronze plaque describing the National Natural Landmark. Immediately, you are surrounded by great trees and fern-covered slopes. Pass massive logs felled in a long-ago storm and notice the lush moss carpets.

In 1.25 miles, pass the first trail on your left. The main trail leaves the virgin forest and enters Tall Timbers Natural Area, which was selectively cut in 1900. This trail continues for 2 miles. Walk a bit farther before returning the way you came.

This time, take the side trail to your right up Thick Mountain. At the top, the trail descends sharply and reaches Swift Run Road. Turn left to reach the picnic area.

■ CONTACT INFORMATION

Bald Eagle State Forest, P.O. Box 147, Laurelton, Pennsylvania 17835, 570-922-3344

13. WOODBOURNE FOREST SANCTUARY

With 100 acres of primeval forest located on a 654-acre property the Cope Family donated to the Nature Conservancy in 1956, Woodbourne Sanctuary is the ideal place to see what the forest looked like before William Penn's time.

Walking among shaggy hemlocks up to 427 years old and 52 inches in diameter and venerable northern red oaks 48 inches thick, you'll feel you've traveled back in time. Other veterans to spot include sugar and red maple, yellow and black birch, black cherry, white ash, and American beech.

In northeast Pennsylvania, take I-81 to Exit 67. Follow signs to New Milford, where you take Route 706 south 9 miles to Montrose. At a traffic light, turn left on Route 29 and drive 5.3 miles south. On your left is the parking lot, marked by a prominent sign.

■ **HIGHLIGHTS**

Pick up a trail guide and follow the yellow trail. At the meadow, look for a yellow post in the middle, then look for an obscure orange blaze on trees at the edge of the meadow. Follow the orange trail from here on.

The self-guided tour takes you through only a small portion of the primeval forest. For an in-depth look at the old growth, contact the sanctuary manager in advance for a guided tour of the unmarked trail network.

■ **CONTACT INFORMATION**

Woodbourne Forest Sanctuary, R.D. 6, Box 6294, Montrose, Pennsylvania 18801, 570-278-3384

14. Salt Springs State Park

The real treasure of 411-acre Salt Springs State Park is a 20-acre ancient forest framing waterfalls that cascade between walls of shale. Here you will see 440-year-old hemlocks and other elders possibly between 600 and 700 years old.

The park is named after its curious natural salt spring. Native Americans closely guarded its artesian well as a rare source of salt. Nearby are historic buildings dating back to the 1840s.

■ **DIRECTIONS**

In northeast Pennsylvania, take I-81 to Exit 67. Follow signs to New Milford and take Route 706 for 9 miles to Montrose. From here, take Route 29 north 7 miles to Franklin Forks. Immediately after a bridge, turn left onto Route 4008 and drive 0.9 mile until you see a small sign and a steep driveway to your left. Enter the park here.

■ **HIGHLIGHTS**

From the parking lot, walk across the creek at the picnic area. See the springs to your left at the base of the hill. Consult the large wall map and use the trail map. Take the Hemlock Trail up the left side of the brook. Climb the trail up to each of the three cascades and admire the ancient hemlocks on the slopes. At the top, the trail heads up to the left, into the woods. Take the next left-hand trail through ancient forest. Also take trails to your right to loop through more of the park.

■ **CONTACT INFORMATION**

Salt Springs State Park, P.O. Box 541, Montrose, Pennsylvania 18801, 570-967-7275

15. DINGMANS FALLS AND DEER LEAP FALLS

Sometimes the best things come in pairs. On the Pennsylvania side of 70,000-acre Delaware Water Gap National Recreation Area, Dingmans Falls boasts a virgin forest of stocky and twisted hemlocks. Only 2 miles up the same stream, 400- and 500-year-old hemlocks hang over Deer Leap Falls.

These falls, best seen in spring, are worth a visit in their own right: Dingmans, Pennsylvania's second tallest, spills more than 100 feet, while Silverthread falls 80 feet through a spectacular chute. To see rhododendron and mountain laurel at peak blossom from the trail, visit in June or July.

Nearby Deer Leap, Fulmer, and Factory Falls (accessible through the George Childs Recreation Site), are rimmed by ledges and wooden walkways surrounded by enormous white pines and hemlocks. As the rush of plunging water fills the air, be sure to inhale the sweetly pungent aroma of white pines and hemlock. Visit the falls in winter for a chance to see some of the Northeast's most magical ice formations.

■ DIRECTIONS AND HIGHLIGHTS

From I-80 on the Pennsylvania side of Delaware Water Gap, take the exit for Route 209 north. Drive 6 miles to the park's visitor center at Bushkill and get maps for both sets of falls. Continue 12 miles farther to the sign for Dingmans Falls at Johnny Bee Road. The trail to Dingmans Falls is an easy boardwalk up stairs to the top of the falls.

To reach Deer Leap Falls, follow directions for Dingmans Falls, then take Route 209 north. Turn left on Route 739. In 1.2 miles, turn left onto Silver Lake Road. Cross Milford Road and drive 0.3 mile farther. Turn left into George Childs Recreation Site. First walk upstream to see Factory Falls, the site of an 1825 wool mill. Then take trails downstream to other cascades and impressive trees

■ CONTACT INFORMATION

Delaware Water Gap National Recreation Area, HQ, River Road off Route 209, Bushkill, Pennsylvania 18324, 570-588-2435

16. HENRY'S WOODS

William Henry may have been one of the Revolutionary War's largest makers of firearms, but he also appreciated the beauty of nature. Henry spared a 40-acre grove of ancient trees on his estate, which is now part of the state's 1,168-acre Jacobsburg Environmental Education Center.

Henry's Woods includes a flat forest along a placid curve of Bushkill Creek and a ferny wall of hemlock, white pine, sugar maple, yellow and black birch, and northern red, white, and chestnut oak. Some reach more than 36 inches in diameter and are 180 to 350 years old.

■ DIRECTIONS

From Bethlehem, take Route 33 north to the Belfast exit. Turn right at the end of the exit. At Belfast Road, turn left (west), drive 0.7 mile (passing under Route 33) and turn left into the park.

■ HIGHLIGHTS

Pick up a trail map and head to the end of the parking lot, where you cross the bridge over the creek to the 2-mile orange trail. Admire the ancient forest on the river terrace and compare it to the cliff and virgin forest on the opposite shore. At 0.4 mile, enjoy the view from the 40-foot cliff of Indian Lookout. Leaving the old forest, walk straight ahead and arrive at the Boulton Visitor Center on your left.

Cross the creek to visit the historic Henry homes and the 1830 champion English elms. Now walk upstream. Take the second trail (orange) on your right. Climb uphill and reenter ancient woods. For the next 0.4 mile, overlook the very steep, hemlock-clothed slopes with the creek far below. Ancient oaks join the hemlocks. Examine the bent, gnarled, stag-headed, and buttress-rooted trunks that give old-growth trees so much more character than those in second-growth woods. After enjoying the area, descend and return to your car.

■ CONTACT INFORMATION

Jacobsburg Environmental Education Center, 835 Jacobsburg Road, Wind Gap, Pennsylvania 18091, 610-746-2801

17. KELLY'S RUN AND OTTER CREEK

Wilderness coexists with industry at Kelly's Run and Otter Creek, two neighboring preserves owned by Pennsylvania Power & Light. But you wouldn't realize it walking beneath the giant 300-year-old hemlocks and shaggy pillars of tulip trees and sycamores. In these two utterly wild canyons, crystal cascades pour into emerald pools, and sparkling boulders lie jumbled with ferns, toppled trees, and luxuriant rhododendrons. Yet only a mile away is PP&L's Holtwood Hydroelectric Dam on the Susquehanna River.

Up to 65 acres of ancient forest are protected in Kelly's Run, with as much as 200 acres at Otter Creek. Visit Otter Creek in May for what may be the Northeast's largest stand of umbrella magnolia, which bloom with giant white flowers and 2-foot-wide leaves that look like they belong in the tropics.

■ DIRECTIONS

Start from Lancaster and take Route 272 south for 13 miles. Turn right at Route 372. For Kelly's Run, drive 4.8 miles on Route 372 and turn right on River Road. At 2.2 miles, turn left on Pinnacle Road and drive to its end. Park at Pinnacle Overlook.

For Otter Creek, take Route 372 south for 9.2 miles (across the Susquehanna). Turn right onto Route 74 and drive 3.3 miles. Turn right on Route 425 and go 4.2 miles to the parking area for Otter Creek.

▪ HIGHLIGHTS

For Kelly's Run, walk the Conestoga Trail south from the overlook for 0.7 mile to Kelly's Run Brook. Turn left and walk a half mile upstream through the gorge. The Pinnacle Trail cuts off to your left and returns to your car in three-quarters of a mile.

For Otter Creek, get a map at the campground office and take the 1.5-mile red-blazed Otter Creek Trail next to the bridge. Follow it through the gorge. Upstream, it crosses the creek, where it leaves the red trail and heads through younger woods back to your car.

▪ CONTACT INFORMATION

Pennsylvania Power & Light, 800-354-8383

18. FERNCLIFF PRESERVE

In the aptly named Ferncliff Preserve, abundant ferns adorn glistening cliffs along a sparkling stream. The preserve's 30 acres include old-growth northern red oak up to 5 feet thick, hemlock, tulip tree, and white oak. Springtime showcases redbud, rhododendron, mountain laurel, and other wildflower displays. In 1972, Congress designated this Lancaster County Conservancy preserve a National Natural Landmark.

From Lancaster take Route 272 south and head right on Chestnut Hill Road. At River Road, take a left. Take the first right onto Slate Hill Road, then right on Benton Hollow Road, and right onto Bald Eagle Road. Park where you see the Lancaster County Conservancy sign and a gated road.

■ HIGHLIGHTS

Head down the woods road for a pleasant, easy walk through the glen to the shore of the great Susquehanna River.

■ CONTACT INFORMATION

Lancaster County Conservancy, P.O. Box 716, Lancaster, Pennsylvania 17608, 717-392-7891

19. THE PEAK FOREST

Huge tulip trees, as well as large beech and northern red oaks, add their stately beauty to this 7-acre suburban Philadelphia preserve owned by Pennypack Ecological Restoration Trust. The grove is a mix of secondary old growth and a few possible original survivors, with trees ranging from 160 to 210 years. It is named for the peaked pile of boulders at the top of the knoll in the woods.

■ DIRECTIONS

Take Pennsylvania Turnpike to Exit 27. Head south a half mile on Route 611. Turn left and drive 2.1 miles on Fitzwatertown Road (the name changes to Terwood Road after crossing Route 263). Turn left on Edgehill Road. In 0.3 mile, watch for the entrance to Pennypack Trust's visitor center.

At the visitor center, inquire about public tours or ask for a map and trail directions to Peak Forest. For a shorter walk, drive back to Terwood Road and turn left. Drive 1.2 miles, then turn left onto Creek Road and drive to its end. Walk on the gated woods road (Creek Road Trail). In 300 feet, turn left onto the Peak Trail. After passing large tulip trees and red oaks up the hill, take the first right and then bear right on the Management Trail spur to return back down to Creek Road Trail. Turn right onto Creek Road Trail to return to your car.

■ CONTACT INFORMATION

Pennypack Ecological Restoration Trust, 2955 Edgehill Road, Huntingdon Valley, Pennsylvania 19006, 215-657-0830

20. WISSAHICKON VALLEY PARK

Wissahickon Valley Park is a testament to the ability of nature to heal, if given a chance. The site of mills in the eighteenth century, this deep valley in northwest Philadelphia was turned into a 1,800-acre public park in 1868. Today, secondary old-growth forest 120 to 200 years old grows in many places along the creek.

Old tulip trees, 32 to 42 inches thick, grow with old hemlock, black birch, and rhododendron along the creek corridor. Ancient black birch, sizable sycamore, beech, and northern red, black, white, and chestnut oak also grow in small clusters or scattered throughout the mature forest. The picturesque setting also features a cliff-lined creek, old stone arched bridges, a covered bridge, caves, the Devils Pool, statues, and historic buildings.

■ **DIRECTIONS**

From downtown Philadelphia, take I-76 (Schuylkill Expressway) west to Exit 32. Follow Lincoln Drive 2.5 miles to McCallum Street (eighth traffic light). Turn left, go a mile, and cross a bridge. Jog right onto Mermaid Lane. In a quarter mile, turn left onto St. Martins Street. Turn left in two blocks onto Springfield Avenue. Bear right at the fork to Valley Green Road. Drive to its end, cross the creek, and park.

■ **HIGHLIGHTS**

Walk back over the stone bridge and take the first trail on your left. Make a left at the first trail fork. Follow this orange-blazed trail along the creek. In a half mile, you see the first clusters of large tulip tree, hemlock, and red, white, and black oaks, especially to your left. At a dead-end woods road, cross an artistic stone bridge and ascend the steps. Following the shore trail, you pass scattered large trees and a delightful, red covered bridge.

Continue along the river without crossing the bridge to see spectacular tulip trees. In three-quarters of a mile, cross Dells Mill Bridge. Turn left on Forbidden Drive past the covered bridge and huge riverside trees, all the way back to your car. You can also hike to the gorge's other end to see more magnificent trees and scenery.

■ **CONTACT INFORMATION**

Friends of the Wissahickon, 8708 Germantown Avenue, Philadelphia, Pennsylvania 19118, 215-247-0417

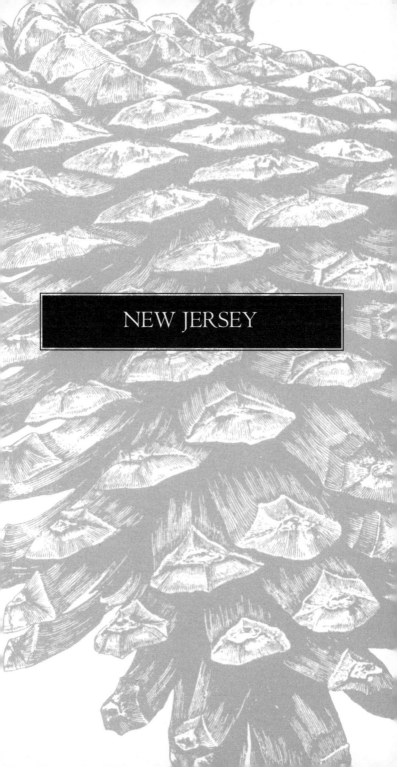

NEW JERSEY

The dense development and long history of forest clearing in New Jersey lead many to believe no old growth survived. European settlers started clearing the forests in the mid-1600s, and during the Revolutionary War, battles fought in New Jersey intensified forest cutting for military purposes. Situated between New York City and Philadelphia, New Jersey's woodlands fell to agriculture and, later, urban sprawl.

Yet some ancient forests survived, and in the most improbable places. One of the state's finest groves is wedged between New Jersey Turnpike and Route 1. Others stand atop the Palisades Cliff across from New York City, on an island in the Delaware River, on the Atlantic beachfront, and next to an industrial suburb. Most remarkably, New Jersey boasts one of the East Coast's oldest hardwood forests, Bear Swamp West, with champion black gums 380 to 500 years old.

Today, most of New Jersey's ancient groves are permanently protected, but the acreage is small. The state's fourteen known ancient groves total only 650 acres, or 0.03 of 1 percent of the state's total forest. Most of the old growth is in the northern part of the state. Southern New Jersey's best-known woodland, the million-acre Pine Barrens, has no known old growth.

However, the search conducted for this book appears to be the first formal statewide survey of New Jersey's old growth. Most of the state's forest experts still deny that any New Jersey old growth has survived. Some owners and stewards don't even know they harbor old-growth groves. One of New Jersey's most impressive groves is one of our newest discoveries. Given these facts, we are confident more discoveries will be made.

21. SADDLER'S WOODS (MACARTHUR FOREST)

New Jersey's newest old-growth discovery, Saddler's Woods, is also one of its most impressive sites, with 31 acres of tremendous trees, including a champion-size, 300-year-old beech that measures 51 inches in diameter. Here you'll also find 61-inch-thick tulip trees and 4-foot-diameter white, black, scarlet, red, swamp white, and chestnut oaks, all 180 to 250 years old. Other senior citizens include sweet gum, shagbark hickory, black cherry, and red maple.

This ancient forest has a unique history. Joshua Saddler, a freed black slave who owned the land in the 1840s, stated in his will that heirs could not cut it down. The state purchased it in the early 1990s to protect the woods from a developer. For years, Saddler's Woods was threatened by the town's plans to build an athletic field on part of the woods. Fortunately, an intense citizen campaign resulted in permanent protection for the town's portion of the woods in April 2003.

■ **DIRECTIONS**

Take New Jersey Turnpike to Exit 3. Take Route 168 (Blackhorse Turnpike) a mile north, passing Route 295. Go another 0.6 mile, turn right, and go 1.6 miles on Kings Highway. Turn left on Crystal Lake Road and, after 1 mile, turn left on MacArthur Boulevard. The trail into the woods is on the left after the third block on the right (Briarwood).

■ **HIGHLIGHTS**

Follow the wide trail and take the first right. After crossing a brook, pass a trail to the left. Continue uphill to the champion beech. Then return to the side trail and turn right. Look on the right, toward an athletic field fence, for the giant tulip trees. Shortly after, the trail veers left and crosses the brook. At the next trail junction, look for the champion chestnut oak. After veering left, the trail continues a quarter mile back to MacArthur Boulevard.

■ **CONTACT INFORMATION**

Newton Creek Watershed Association, P.O. Box 484, Collingwood, New Jersey 08108, 856-854-5693

22. HELYAR WOODS

Great, grooved, 250-year-old oaks fill Helyar Woods, which is wedged between Route 1 and the New Jersey Turnpike. The 30-acre woods features twenty-three tree species, including twelve that are old growth. Ancient white, black, northern red, scarlet, and swamp white oaks dominate, with diameters of 30 to 45 inches. Aged American beech, black birch, black cherry, and shagbark hickory grow with sweet gum and red maple. Black gum are possibly 300 years or older. Scattered American holly are the only evergreens in this forest, and umbrella magnolia is the most unusual tree species.

Helyar Woods resides in Rutgers University's Horticultural Gardens, whose officials first learned of its old-growth status when we performed our survey for this book. The gardens' director told us there is no historical evidence of cutting.

■ DIRECTIONS

Take New Jersey Turnpike to Exit 9. Follow Route 18 toward New Brunswick. At the next exit, take Route 1 south to its next exit, Ryders Lane. Head south on Ryders Lane to the first left into Rutgers Gardens, then turn left on Log Cabin Road and take it through the gardens to its end. Park near the log cabin. The forest is on your left.

■ HIGHLIGHTS

Pick up a trail guide. The trail starts at the Helyar Monument. Veer left on the trail, then make the first right. You may wish to take the short loop trail to your left into the wetland. The main trail exits the old growth, following the edge of a field. Turn right and pass through a beautiful tunnel of planted pines. The trail swings rightward back through ancient oaks, 180 to 260 years old. Observe the deeply furrowed, shaggy, or balding antique bark. Along a lake, the trail descends into a ravine with a small cascade and a red shale cliff, before returning to the parking area.

After you visit the woods, see the rest of Rutgers Gardens, including one of the world's largest collections of American holly.

■ **CONTACT INFORMATION**

Rutgers Gardens, Rutgers University, 112 Ryders Lane, New Brunswick, New Jersey 08901, 732-932-8451

23. BULL'S ISLAND

Bull's Island, squeezed between the Delaware and Raritan Canal and the Delaware River, features an incredibly rare old-growth floodplain forest. Columns of 5-foot-thick sycamore, 42-inch-thick silver maple, and 52-inch-thick tulip tree rise up to 140 feet in these woods. Silver maple of this size is unusual, as this species is typically short-lived. Grape vines 12 inches thick are so large they resemble shaggy bent trunks. Other unusual trees are river birch and honey locust.

Completed in 1834 and closed in 1932, the 66-mile Delaware and Raritan Canal separates Bull's Island from New Jersey's mainland. Why this forest wasn't cut down when the canal was built is a mystery. The island and canal became a State Park in 1974 and a National Recreation Trail in 1992.

■ **DIRECTIONS**

Take the New Jersey Turnpike to Exit 10 onto Route 287 North. Exit onto Route 202 and drive west and south. At the Delaware River, go 6 miles north on Route 29. Turn left into

Bull's Island Park. Park on the left side of the lot, near the nature trail on the canal side of the island.

■ **HIGHLIGHTS**

The 0.9-mile trail follows the canal to the island's end. Return on the path along the river's side and detour onto the Delaware River footbridge for a scenic view. Next, visit the campground on the north side of the island. Look on your right for two colossal, reclining sycamores between the road and the canal. Scattered, huge black oaks and silver maples grow near the campground, along with large, uncommon hackberries.

■ **CONTACT INFORMATION**

Delaware and Raritan Canal State Park, 2185 Daniel Bray Highway, Stockton, New Jersey 08559, 609-397-2949

24. HUTCHESON MEMORIAL FOREST

Until very recently, the 65-acre Hutcheson Memorial Forest was the only documented ancient forest in New Jersey. Research confirms that some of its oaks germinated as long ago as 1627.

White oaks ranging in age from 330 to 400 years and black oaks with 30- to 42-inch diameters grow straight as arrows, scattered in the open woods. Other ancients are shagbark hickory, sugar maple, beech, red maple, flowering dogwood, red oak, black gum, and mockernut hickory. The rare persimmon tree grows here, too. Unfortunately, blowdown areas have been invaded by dense colonies of foreign plants, breaking up the once-closed primeval canopy.

Although original settlers chose not to cut this forest, the owners decided to log it in the 1950s. Committed citizens and a carpenters union rallied and raised the money to save it. In 1955, it became one of the first projects of the Nature Conservancy. In the late 1960s, Congress recognized it as a National Natural Landmark. Now owned by Rutgers University, the forest is a 400-acre ecology research station just east of Millstone.

■ **CONTACT INFORMATION**

Only guided tours are allowed, through the Hutcheson Memorial Forest, Department of Ecology, Evolution and Natural Resources, Rutgers University, New Brunswick, New Jersey 08903, 732-932-9631.

25. DELAWARE WATER GAP

Millions of people drive through Delaware Water Gap with no idea that the jagged 1,300-foot cliffs of Kittatinny Mountain harbor clusters of ancient hemlock, pine, and black birch. From river level, the ancient trees look scrubby, but up close, they are highly picturesque, contorted trees. They range in age from 150 to 300 years.

■ **DIRECTIONS**

Take I-80 to Exit 1 on the New Jersey side of the highway and follow signs to the visitor center.

Ask for directions to Dunnfield Creek Natural Area and to the Appalachian Trail, which you can take to the tops of Mounts Tammany and Minsi. From here you can see the awesome cliffs, panoramas, and craggy, bonsai-like trees. Bring binoculars.

■ CONTACT INFORMATION

Delaware Water Gap National Recreation Area, Kittatinny Point Visitor Center, off Route 80, Columbia, New Jersey 07832, 570-588-2435

26. TILLMAN RAVINE

Hemlocks 130 to 200 years old, 112 feet high, and 40 inches in diameter grow in the 25-acre grove of Tillman Ravine with red oak and sugar maple. Rhododendron and mountain laurel create a deep-shaded, evergreen ambiance. There has been little to no selective cutting since the 1800s.

Exquisite Tillman Brook tumbles over two cascades and the Tea Cup, a stream-carved pothole in this 500-acre Natural Area in Stokes State Forest on the state's highest ridge, Kittatinny Mountain.

■ DIRECTIONS

From New York City, take I-80 west to Exit 34. Drive 20 miles northwest on Route 15, then northwest on Route 206 for 8.5 miles. Pass the State Forest office, then turn left on Struble Road (later called Dimon Road, then Brink Road) at the sign for Kittatinny Boy Scout Camp. Drive

west 4.3 miles. Turn left at the parking lot for Upper Falls
Parking Area.

■ **HIGHLIGHTS**

From the south side of the lot, take the main trail south to
Tillman Brook. The trail follows the brook through old forest, passing Upper Falls. At 0.8 mile, reach Lower Falls and
the Tea Cup. Return the way you came.

■ **CONTACT INFORMATION**

Stokes State Forest, 1 Coursen Road, Branchville, New Jersey 07826, 973-948-3820

27. JOCKEY HOLLOW

It's not hard to imagine Revolutionary War soldiers roaming
the tall tulip tree forests of Jockey Hollow. After all, it was
the wood lot next to the encampment for 10,000 starving,
freezing soldiers from 1779 to 1780. (Washington slept in
a mansion 4 miles away.) Today, the hollow is part of the
Morristown National Historical Park.

Up to 100 acres of secondary old-growth forest has grown
here since that time. Tulip trees are now 130 to 220 years
old, 24 to 42 inches in diameter, and 120 feet tall. Historical research indicates that the site had selective cutting until
the mid-1800s.

■ **DIRECTIONS**

Take I-287 to Exit 30B. Go 2 miles north on Route 202.
Turn left on Tempe Wick Road. Go 1.5 miles to the entrance
and visitor center.

■ **HIGHLIGHTS**

Pick up a trail map and ask the ranger to direct you to this trail route: from the visitor center, take a right onto Mendham Road, a left onto the orange Grand Loop Trail (through a half mile of ancient forest), a left on Red Trail, a right on Jockey Hollow Road, and a left on the yellow Grand Parade Trail to Wick Farm and Wick House (1750). Return to the parking lot just down from Jockey Hollow Road.

■ **CONTACT INFORMATION**

Morristown National Historical Park, Washington Place, Morristown, New Jersey 07960, 973-543-4030

28. JENKINS WOODS

Stately oaks and maples create a pretty setting in the 20-acre Helen Hartley Jenkins Woods on the Loantaka Brook Reservation. Largely undisturbed for the last two centuries, this lowland old-growth forest includes 3-foot-thick white oaks up to 300 years old, beeches 200 to 300 years old, and 40-inch-diameter tulip trees that grow to 120 feet tall.

■ **DIRECTIONS**

Take I-287 to Morristown to Exit 35. If southbound, turn right onto South Street; if northbound, turn right onto Madison Avenue, drive 0.1 mile to a traffic light, and turn left onto South Street. Immediately take the left fork onto Woodland Avenue. Drive 1.2 miles to Kitchell Road and turn right. In a quarter mile, turn right into Loantaka Reservation.

The Blue Trail starts on the other side of Kitchell Road, across from the parking lot. The old forest begins a quarter mile after a footbridge over Loantaka Brook. For the next quarter mile, pass through Jenkins Woods. Old forest ends when the trail passes between two sections of a fence. Go a little farther, turn right, then turn right again onto a bridle trail, which continues through the old woods back to Kitchell Road. Cross the road and follow the trail around the lake to your car.

■ CONTACT INFORMATION

Morris County Park Commission, P.O. Box 1295, East Hanover Avenue, Morristown, New Jersey 07962, 973-326-7600

29. LAUREL POND

Laurel Pond is in the middle of 13,000-acre Wawayanda State Park, which covers rugged, rocky hills along the border with New York State. Although it's only 5 acres in size, the primitive grove on Laurel Pond looks like it belongs in the Adirondacks—except for the dense evergreen rhododendrons. Three-foot-thick hemlocks crowd rocky, moss-green ledges of the southeast shore of the pond.

■ DIRECTIONS

Take I-287 in New Jersey to Exit 52. Proceed 7 miles west on Route 23. Exit onto Union Valley Road (Route 513) north and drive 6 miles to a stop sign. Go to the second traffic light and turn left. Drive 2 miles to a fork in the road and veer left. Drive a half mile to Warwick Turnpike and turn left. Go 4 miles to the park entrance, on the left. Get a trail map and drive to the last parking lot at Wawayanda Lake.

■ **HIGHLIGHTS**

With the lake on your right, head east on the yellow Double Pond Trail. In a quarter mile, pass historic iron furnace ruins. Stay to the right, on the yellow trail (now called Laurel Pond Trail). In a quarter mile, turn right on the trail to Laurel Pond. At the pond, look to your left (southeast) at the old-growth evergreens hugging the shore bluff in the distance. There is no formal trail. Follow along the top of the bluff, climbing through rhododendrons.

Return back to the main trail and take a left turn to return. Alternatively, take a right turn and walk 1 mile to the Cedar Swamp Trail, which cuts through a rare, old-growth inland Atlantic white cedar swamp.

■ **CONTACT INFORMATION**

Wawayanda State Park, P.O. Box 198, Highland Lakes, New Jersey 07422, 973-853-4462

WESTERN NEW YORK
and the
FINGER LAKES REGION

New York may have the largest population of any eastern state, as well as the nation's largest city, but surprisingly, it also claims the Northeast's largest area of old-growth forest—almost 400,000 acres. In fact, New York's old growth comprises 2.2 percent of the state's total forest land. This is not because its forests were too rugged for logging, nor is it because the state intended to protect its last virgin trees. Rather, it is because of a simple, historical quirk: New York City needed drinking water.

After the Civil War, New York City experienced a population boom, forcing city planners to quickly secure a reliable water supply. Since large, intact forests yield the most sustained and clean sources, planners looked to the Catskills and Adirondacks. In the late 1880s, the state legislature voted to establish forest preserves that were made permanent by the state constitution in 1894. Today, the Adirondacks contain between 250,000 and 500,000 acres of unlogged (or minimally logged) lands, which is 98 percent of the state's old growth. This is distributed over about 70 large parcels. The state's remaining 5,000 acres are scattered among approximately 110 separate stands.

Of properties in New York that harbor ancient forests, only Fire Island is National Park land. The state owns 20 percent of old-growth properties, 20 percent are local parks, and nonprofit nature preserves own 25 percent. The remaining 35 percent are still privately owned and have no permanent protection. Two Indian reservations possess four small, unprotected groves. (Because formal old-growth surveys have only just begun for most of the state, these statistics are all preliminary.)

New York's old-growth diversity is amazing: towering pine forests; dwarf holly, subalpine spruce, and cliff cedars; as well as small urban groves and vast landscapes of primeval forest. Unfortunately, there is no formal protection for old growth in New York state. Because of this, a number of major environmental battles in western New York and the Finger Lakes region have been aimed at saving these majestic forests and surrounding wildlands. These efforts are justified: this region is famous for dramatic scenic features, including Niagara Falls, Letchworth Gorge (the deepest vertical-walled canyon in the east), Allegany State Park (one of the country's largest state parks), Lake Ontario and Lake Erie (two of the world's largest lakes), and of course, the fourteen Finger Lakes. The area is also known for the awe-inspiring Gallery of Giants old-growth forest. Downstream from Niagara Falls, the Niagara Gorge ancient cedars—which are up to 750 or more years old—form one of the oldest tree communities in the east.

Western New York is one of only two areas in the Northeast that has been comprehensively surveyed for old growth. In 1983, author Bruce Kershner became the first to look for old growth in this region. (At the same time, author Robert Leverett began his survey of Massachusetts, the Northeast's only other extensively surveyed area.) In 1989, Kershner cofounded the Western New York Old Growth Forest Survey, a team of volunteers that has discovered sixty-six ancient forests to date. Their work has inspired the formation of survey teams in central and eastern New York, as well as in the Adirondacks.

Unlike western New York, the Finger Lakes region outside of the Syracuse area has not been extensively surveyed for old growth. Only six sites have been confirmed in an area the size of Vermont. Around Syracuse, however, survey teams have found eight sites, including the Wizard of Oz Grove.

The extensive surveys of western New York have made it possible to document how ancient forests are distributed and why they survived. About one-third of properties with old growth were former estates or lakeside vacation cottage sites. One in four stands is on park land that was acquired before loggers arrived. Another quarter grow on sites that were inaccessible or too steep for old-fashioned logging methods. About 18 percent of the stands are on private lands settled by people whose descendants have carried on a tradition of preservation. Surprisingly, 40 percent of the sites are within or adjacent to urban areas, while 35 percent are found in wilder forested hill country. About 25 percent are in agricultural regions.

30. ZOAR VALLEY CANYON

Zoar Valley Canyon features the Gallery of Giants, the East's tallest hardwood forest outside of the Great Smoky Mountains. It is also New York's largest virgin forest outside the Adirondacks and includes a spectacular array of other highlights: a 15-mile canyon, twenty waterfalls, knife-edge ridges, and white-water rafting. Zoar Valley's public lands and preserves hold 615 acres of old growth; another 150 acres are unprotected private lands.

Gnarly hemlocks up to 500 years old line the canyon's 400-foot virgin slopes and rim. The rim hemlocks attain fantastic bonsai or daredevil shapes, sometimes jutting out 40 feet over the canyon. Along one of the walking routes, America's champion 300-year-old wild grape vine reaches 14 inches in diameter and a quarter mile in length.

At the bottom of the canyon, the Gallery of Giants is a 5-mile stretch of 32- to 50-inch-diameter trees, 150 to 350 years old. At 120 to 150 feet tall, the trees here form the tallest broadleaf forest in the Northeast. This area also boasts the world's tallest American basswood (128.7 feet) and American elm (123 feet), the world's second tallest sycamore (155 feet), and the East's tallest broadleaf outside of the Smokies, a 156-foot tulip tree.

As perhaps the Northeast's most diverse old-growth forest, Zoar Valley Canyon boasts twenty-five ancient tree species. The most common are hemlock, sugar maple, tulip tree, sycamore, and northern red oak. Rare species include American elm and cucumber magnolia.

Although most of the old growth is on state land, none of it is protected from state logging efforts. A recent citizen campaign prevented state logging plans along the canyon, but a new plan is being written.

■ **DIRECTIONS**

Take New York Thruway (I-90), west of Buffalo, to Exit 58. Turn right onto Routes 5 and 20 east. In a mile, cross Cattaraugus Creek, turn right, and drive 12.2 miles on Route 438. Turn right on Route 62 south. Cross the bridge over Cattaraugus Creek in downtown Gowanda, and immediately turn left on Water Street.

Follow Water Street (changing names to Commercial and Palmer streets). Turn right on Broadway. At the top of the hill, turn left on Point Peter Road, just after you pass a white concrete wall. Go less than a mile and turn left onto dirt Valentine Flats Road. Drive to its dead end and park.

■ **HIGHLIGHTS**

The memorable 3-mile round-trip hike to Point Peter and the Gallery of Giants can be done only in the summer. From the parking area, walk on the dirt road through the dead-end barrier. Ignore the first left-hand woods road. At the fork just after that, take the path on the left through old growth for 1,500 feet. You reach Point Peter, a knife-edge ridge with a breathtaking panoramic view. Caution: going near the edge is dangerous.

Return to the trail fork and follow the woods road down into the canyon. At the bottom, take the first left trail through a thicket and then take a right fork through a walnut plantation. Ignore a small path on the right in the thicket. When it reenters woods, turn right on the trail fork. Pass through Grape Alley, named for large tangles of grape vines some 150 years old.

At the bluff over the creek, skirt the edge of the creek's bank. At the end of the peninsula, climb down the bank of the creek. You are now at Skinny Dip Beach, where South Branch joins Main Cattaraugus Creek. Admire Great Sculpted Cliff towering 380 feet above you. Carefully ford South Branch Creek (summer only), then pass to the left under the jutting, prominent cliff. Hike upstream along the south shore of the Main Branch. In 500 feet, as soon as you reach the wooded terrace on the right, cut into the woods.

When the path veers away from the canyon slope and you enter mature forest, walk off-trail through the woods along the bottom of the steep slope, keeping it on your right. You are now in the Gallery of Giants. Look up to get a sense of the trees' soaring trunks. These trees are so high, you will have difficulty seeing their lowest boughs. Here you will see the tallest hardwood tree in eastern North America outside of the Great Smokies: the 156-foot-high "Skinny Dip Giant." You will also see the Northeast's tallest northern red oak (131 feet), slippery elm (120.4 feet), and bitternut hickory (136.4 feet).

When the river terrace narrows at the gravel island, carefully cross the creek and walk into the forest on the opposite side. Wander upstream through this second terrace, noting the mix of ancient trees. Towering trees are everywhere, including the Northeast's largest beech (with a 47.2-inch diameter) and black walnut, as well as New York's tallest white ash (139 feet), slippery elm (120.4 feet), and sugar maple (124 feet). When the forest terrace ends, return by walking downstream along the shore. You pass opposite 430-foot Giant Fluted Cliff.

Head downstream all the way to where the South Branch joins the Main Branch. Cross the South Branch creek again, but do not climb up the riverbank. Instead, head downstream along the Main Branch. Walk beneath overhanging ledges lined with cliff-hanging ancient hemlocks.

Pass under the barren cliffs of the Valentine Pyramid. When the cliffs end, immediately climb up the riverbank. Do not continue downstream or you'll miss the return trail.

Once atop the bank, take the trail to your left (not right). At the next fork, turn right. When you come to a trail fork in the thicket, bear right. At the next fork, turn left. When you reach the woods road, turn right to ascend the hill. At the top, turn left on the woods road to return to your car.

■ CONTACT INFORMATION

New York Department of Environmental Conservation, 270 Michigan Avenue, Buffalo, New York 14202, 716-851-7200

31. Big Basin of Allegany State Park

Rugged and primeval, the 400-acre Big Basin occupies the heart of New York's largest state park, the 100-square-mile Allegany State Park.

The Big Basin is one of the eastern United States' few tracts with an abundance of large, ancient black cherry (32 to 48 inches in diameter). Growing with them are large hemlock, yellow birch, sugar maple, and northern red oak, mostly 200 to 350 years in age. Sizable red maple, white pine, white ash, basswood, and cucumber magnolia accompany them.

Allegany State Park has another thirteen smaller ancient groves and likely even more ancient forest yet to be documented. The old-growth stands are the state's only original forest that survived destruction by the Ice Age glaciers. Ironically, this forest almost didn't survive human destruction. In 1981, New York's parks department planned to log the Big Basin and the majority of the park. A fourteen-year statewide citizens' campaign convinced Governor Pataki in 1995 to protect the old growth, but 23 percent of the rest of the forest is still open to logging. The Big Basin is also threatened by severe deer overbrowsing and beech blight.

- **DIRECTIONS**

Take I-86 (Route 17) to Exit 19. Follow signs to Allegany State Park and Red House. Follow Park Road #2 to Red House Lake and to the park headquarters. Ask for a park map. Take Park Road #2 a quarter mile along Red House Lake to the first right. Set your odometer. Drive on Park Road #1 exactly 2.1 miles and park at the first stone bridge across a brook.

- **HIGHLIGHTS**

There are no trails in the Big Basin. Bring a compass and prepare for a rugged walk. You will be rewarded for it. For an easy route, walk upstream along the brook for thirty minutes (about 0.75 mile) through exquisite old growth, then cross the stream and walk back along the other side.

For the rugged route, bushwhack downstream from the bridge. Start on the west side of the stream (so the brook is on your right). When you reach a larger brook, turn left and follow it upstream. Do not cross it or follow other streams or you may get lost. Parallel the brook upstream for roughly an hour, heading almost due south. At any point you wish, use your compass to head due east. In a quarter mile, you arrive at Park Road #1. Turn left to return to your car, about a mile north. We suggest you return by walking through the woods within sight of the road embankment (not along the road), so you can pass more magnificent trees.

■ **CONTACT INFORMATION**

Big Basin of Allegany State Park, 2373 Allegany State Park, Route 1, Suite 3, Salamanca, New York 14779, 716-354-9121

32. REINSTEIN WOODS

Eighty acres of majestic beech, black cherry, northern red oak, and yellow birch stand like monuments along the trails of Reinstein Woods.

Trees reach 40 inches in diameter and 150 to 250 years in age. One 40-inch beech, 245 years old and 103 feet tall, is one of the state's largest of that species. Impressive black cherries, 150 to 225 years old and up to 45 inches in diameter, indicate the forest has had no cutting since the late 1800s.

Many of the venerable beeches have historic carvings dating back to the early 1800s, including the initials of the town's first white settler, Alexander Hitchcock, and carvings of animals that could be Seneca clan markings from the mid-1800s. Other remarkable features are stone surveyor monuments from 1798, when the Holland Land Company surveyed the region.

In 1986, Dr. Victor Reinstein donated his 289-acre estate to the state. Today it is an outstanding spot for seeing lily-padded ponds and abundant wildlife, only 1.5 miles from the Buffalo city limits. The woods, while protected from cutting, are deteriorating because of severe overbrowsing by the eighty deer living there.

■ **DIRECTIONS**

Take New York Thruway (I-90) near Buffalo to Exit 52 at Walden Avenue East. At Union Road (Route 277), turn right (south) and drive 1.1 miles. Turn left on Como Park Boulevard and drive 1.8 miles. Turn right on Honorine Drive at the wooden Reinstein Woods sign. Turn left into the entrance gate.

■ **HIGHLIGHTS**

Reinstein Woods is open only for guided tours on most Saturday and Wednesday mornings or by group reservation.

■ **CONTACT INFORMATION**

Reinstein Woods, 77 Honorine Drive, Depew, New York 14043, 716-683-5959

33. DeVeaux Woods and the Niagara Gorge Ancient Cedars

When the first European explorers beheld the great falls of Niagara, they also noted the great forests of oak lining the banks of the gorge. The 10-acre grove of DeVeaux Woods is New York's sole surviving remnant of this great oak forest, and it has since become the first state park in New York established primarily to protect old growth.

Stocky white, black, and northern red oak between 150 and 275 years old dominate this grove. Tree diameters range from 28 to 42 inches. The crowns and trunks show classic old-growth features, stag-headed tops, and buttressed roots. Once part of the large DeVeaux estate, the grove was donated to Niagara University. When its old-growth status was discovered in 1993, Niagara University was about to sell the grove to a developer, who would have destroyed it. Environmentalists convinced university officials to sell it to the state.

The Niagara Gorge, created by Niagara Falls several miles upstream, is only 500 feet away. The gorge harbors northern white cedars, which at possibly 800 years old, are probably the oldest trees in the Northeast. Most of the gorge's 1,300 ancient cedars are 200 to 500 years old. Some grow as close as 75 feet away from the falls.

On the Canadian side of the gorge, 60 acres of ancient hardwood forest fills Niagara Glen Nature Preserve, an impressive terrace covered by colossal boulders, towering sugar maples, white ash, and even sassafras. Its massive tulip trees tower 130 feet and may be Ontario's tallest hardwood trees.

■ DIRECTIONS

Take I-190 north from Buffalo to Niagara Falls to Exit 24 at Witmer Road (Route 31). Follow Route 31 west into the city of Niagara Falls. In 2.25 miles, turn left on Lewiston Road (Route 104). Drive several blocks to the DeVeaux entrance on your right, just before athletic fields and Findlay Drive. Drive to the back of the property, behind several large stone buildings, until you see the forest. Park in the nearest lot.

There is a single trail through the woods, but be sure to wander among the trees off-trail, examining the trunks and crowns of the stocky oaks. Try to imagine what it was like in the 1600s when French explorers first met the Seneca Indians near here.

One quick and easy way to see the ancient cliff cedars is to take the Upper Gorge Trail from Art Park. For directions to this nearby park, inquire at the Niagara Park headquarters. Getting a close-up view is difficult because most grow away from trails on very steep sites.

DeVeaux Woods State Park, 3180 DeVeaux Woods Drive, Niagara Falls, New York 14305, 716-284-5778

34. LILY DALE GROVE

Lily Dale Grove is truly a sacred place. Although it is only 20 acres in size, Lily Dale Grove has the greatest density of giant old-growth broadleaf trees of any small grove in the Northeast. It's no wonder that the Lily Dale Spiritualist Assembly chose this dense concentration of immense trees as its formal outdoor temple. This famous community of mediums and spiritualists, established in the 1870s, uses the grove for sacred ceremonies attended by the public.

At the far end of the 20-acre grove is a worship area at Inspiration Stump, the site of a former giant tree of special significance. America's first formal pet cemetery is in one corner of the grove. The amazingly diverse forest boasts sixteen species of 200- to 250-year-old trees. Northern red oaks reach 56 inches in diameter, champion-size white pines are nearly 145 feet tall, and hemlocks are 45 inches thick. Black cherry trees 43 inches thick and 132 feet tall are among the Northeast's most impressive. Other veterans include sugar and red maple, beech, tulip tree, basswood, yellow birch, cucumber magnolia, black walnut, white ash, and shagbark hickory.

■ DIRECTIONS

Take New York Thruway (I-90) west of Buffalo to Exit 59 at Dunkirk. Head 8 miles south on Route 60. Turn right at the sign for Lily Dale, just before Cassadaga Village. Follow this road to Lily Dale's large, arched entrance gate (entrance fee in summer only). From the gate, immediately turn right. In three blocks, the paved road turns left, but go straight and park. The trail entrance is on your right, marked by the Leo-Lyn Woods sign.

■ HIGHLIGHTS

Shortly after the quarter-mile wheelchair-accessible trail starts, take the left trail to the pet cemetery, then return to the main trail loop.

You can also combine your forest visit with a psychic reading!

■ CONTACT INFORMATION

Lily Dale Assembly, 5 Melrose Park, P.O. Box 248, Lily Dale, New York 14752, 716-595-8721

35. Panama Rocks

Growing in this enchanting moss-lined maze of rock crevices and jumbled boulders are eight species of venerable trees covering 15 acres. The 200- to 300-year-old hemlocks are truly bizarre, with fantastically shaped roots that climb across rock walls in intricate networks or spread open like giant claws or wings. Yellow birches drop root ladders from jagged rocks that are covered with garlands of ferns. Along the trail, you'll also spy 42-inch-thick red maple, and 35- to 45-inch-diameter beech, black cherry, and spiral-twisted sugar maples.

Panama Rocks has been protected as a private scenic attraction since the 1800s.

■ **DIRECTIONS**

Take I-86-Route 17 to Exit 7. Go south for 5.7 miles on Route 33 into the village of Panama. Turn right at the signs for Panama Rocks.

■ **HIGHLIGHTS**

Bring flashlights and camera and be sure to explore every nook and cranny along the loop trail, where you'll find the most fascinating trees and rocks. Try to find the deep cave hidden in one alcove.

The park is open May to October.

■ **CONTACT INFORMATION**

Panama Rocks, 11 Rock Hill Road, P.O. Box 176, Panama, New York 14767, 716-782-2845

36. Pfeiffer Nature Center

At the 738-acre Pfeiffer Nature Center, huge hemlocks dominate 20 to 30 acres of primeval forest, surrounded by 50 acres of very mature forest scattered with old growth. Hemlocks as old as 350 years were the favorite trees of Wendy Knox Lawrence, who donated the land to a nonprofit organization for preservation in 1998. The preserve's other senior citizens are northern red and chestnut oak, beech, black gum, white pine, and cucumber magnolia.

The visitor center, a state historic landmark, is constructed entirely of American chestnut that was harvested in the 1930s when the blight killed every chestnut.

■ **DIRECTIONS**

Take I-86-Route 17 to Exit 26 at Olean. Follow signs to Route 16 south. In Olean, turn left and drive 2.5 miles on Route 417 east (State Street). Turn left on Haskell Road and drive 3 miles. Take the right fork onto Wolf Run Road. Drive 0.6 mile and turn right onto Lillibridge Road. Go 2 miles up a steep hill and around a very sharp bend to the right. Park in the entrance lot, on your left, at the top.

■ **HIGHLIGHTS**

Get a trail map and ask about a tour. Take the trail into the ancient woods, bearing left at the fork onto Griffin Way. The next right loops you through the rest of the old forest. Explore the rest of the trail network.

■ **CONTACT INFORMATION**

Pfeiffer Nature Center, Lillibridge Road, P.O. Box 802, Portville, New York 14770, 716-373-1742

37. Letchworth State Park

At 550 feet, the Genesee Gorge in Letchworth State Park is the deepest vertical-walled canyon in the Northeast. Like Niagara Falls, it's also a good place to see communities of ancient trees growing on its cliffs and ravines.

Perhaps the easiest place to visit is Lower Falls Terrace Woods, a 7-acre parcel of impressive ancient hemlock and sugar maple near the 110-foot Lower Falls. Many trees are taller than the huge falls, with one white ash reported to be more than 130 feet.

The cliffs harbor the most ancient trees. At the Great Bend vista along the west rim, people have marveled for decades at the yawning abyss and great curving layers of canyon walls. Use binoculars to see 500-year-old red cedars attached to those walls. From a distance, these trees look like olive-green bushes, but they are actually 20 to 40 feet tall.

■ **DIRECTIONS**

From New York Thruway (I-90), take I-390 south of Rochester to Dansville Exit. Follow Route 436 west to Portageville. Just after Portageville, turn right into the park's entrance and drive to the office.

■ **HIGHLIGHTS**

Pick up a map and ask about summer naturalist tours. Get directions for Great Bend Overlook and the major waterfalls. Don't miss the historic Glen Iris Inn.

■ **CONTACT INFORMATION**

Letchworth State Park, 1 Letchworth State Park, Castile, New York 14427, 585-493-3600

38. Bentley Woods

Located at the edge of metro Rochester, Bentley Woods provides 23 acres of primitive solitude with ancient hemlock, white pine, and northern white cedar.

Its 200- to 350-year-old trees sport diameters of 30 to 40 inches. It is one of the only sites in New York where ancient white cedar, white pine, and hemlock grow together. Ancient beech and sugar maple also populate this area, which includes a glacial esker ridge and kettle swamp left by the Ice Age glacier 12,000 years ago. The land was donated to the Nature Conservancy in 1963 to save it from being logged.

- **DIRECTIONS AND CONTACT INFORMATION**

Call the Nature Conservancy for permission and directions: 585-546-8030.

39. Washington Woods

One of western New York's newest old-growth discoveries, Washington Woods, was preserved as a city park in 1934 on the 200th anniversary of George Washington's birth. Impressive red, black, and white oaks, 180 to 260 years old, cover this 12-acre grove, located within the city of Rochester. It may have survived cutting because of its location on lands set aside to protect the city's drinking water supply.

- **DIRECTIONS**

Take the New York Thruway (I-90) to Exit 45, then take I-490 north to Rochester. Get off at Exit 19. Turn left onto Culver Road south. Turn left onto Monroe Avenue (Route

35), and quickly turn left onto Highland Avenue. In a half mile, turn left onto Cobbs Hill Drive. In three blocks, turn left onto Nunda Boulevard. Park at the end of the road.

■ **HIGHLIGHTS**

Bear left to circle this easy loop trail. Then visit nearby Tryon Park to see impressive old-growth oaks that blanket the park's hills at the north end. To get there, take Highland Avenue to Winton Road and turn left. In 2.2 miles, turn right onto Tryon Park Road. At its end, enter the park and head north on foot trails to the northernmost hills, where the ancient oaks grow.

■ **CONTACT INFORMATION**

Washington Woods, 400 Dewey Avenue, Rochester, New York 14613, 585-428-6770

40. Green Lakes State Park

Green Lakes State Park claims central New York's showcase ancient forest, discovered by the New York Old Growth Forest Association in 2001. At 1,000 acres, it is also the state's largest ancient forest, outside of the Adirondacks.

Huge sugar maples, up to 50 inches thick, grow with 180- to 450-year-old hemlocks and soaring tulip trees, along with yellow birch, beech, white pine, basswood, white ash, bitternut hickory, and the rare chinkapin oak. Even ancient northern white cedars grow along the lakeshores. The park is a cache of stately trees. It has one of the state's tallest broadleaf forests, with trees that average 118 feet in height. The Tulip Tree Cathedral south of Green Lake has trees that reach 145 feet. The lowest bough of one white ash is at the record height of 100 feet.

For decades, people have admired this park's grand forests and meromictic lakes—pristine lakes with deep, aqua-colored, glacial waters that do not mix or turn over each season.

■ DIRECTIONS

Take New York Thruway (I-90) to Exit 34A. Take Route 481 south 1.4 miles, then head 1.3 miles east on Kirkville Road. Turn right on Fremont Road for 1.2 miles, then turn left onto Route 290 for 1.8 miles to the junction with Route 257. Make a left to stay on 290 and continue 1.9 miles to the park entrance. Stop at the park office for a trail map. Follow signs to Green Lake and park at the beach.

■ HIGHLIGHTS

Start at the beach concession building for this 5-mile route. Follow Green Lake Trail along the east side of the lake. From here on, you are in old growth, including shoreline cedars. Turn left at the footbridge at the end of the lake. At the pump house at Round Lake, turn left and circle the lake. At the other end, turn left up a ravine to a trail junction at a footbridge. Head to the left, off-trail, into the Tulip Tree Cathedral. The grove ends at a power line clearing and a groomed bike trail. Turn right on this trail and take another right at the next trail. At the footbridge, take the trail down the ravine. Turn left at Round Lake. Follow the shore back to the pump house and turn left. At the footbridge at Green Lake, turn left to see central New York's champion white pine (130 feet tall, 32.6 inches in diameter). Go around the west shore, passing old growth, almost back to the beach.

Green Lakes State Park, 7900 Green Lakes Road, Fayette-ville, New York 13066, 315-637-6111

41. THE WIZARD OF OZ GROVE

Toward evening they came to a great forest, where the trees grew so big and close together that their branches met over the road of yellow brick. It was almost dark under the trees, for the branches shut out the daylight.

There may not be a yellow brick road through the 7-acre Wizard of Oz Grove of North Syracuse Junior High School, but many people believe it is a remnant of the ancient forest that inspired L. Frank Baum to write the passage above about the journey of Dorothy and her friends through the great forest in *The Wonderful Wizard of Oz*. Baum grew up only a short distance from it in the 1870s and is believed to have roamed the forest as a child. It is also likely that he got the idea of the yellow brick road from the street he lived on. Built in 1846, it was America's first plank road, built of a yellowish hemlock wood.

It is fitting that the grove was saved for, and by, the children of North Syracuse Junior High. Together with old-growth forest sleuths Tom Howard and Robert Henry, students convinced the school board not to cut it down to build athletic fields. The grove now has plaques on the trees named after famous people. The L. Frank Baum Tree is a 150-year-old, 98-foot-tall red oak. Other giants include a pair of 180-year-olds, the Edgar Allan Poe Tree (at 46.2 inches in diameter, a county black oak champion) and the 35.5-inch-thick John Muir Tree. The 160-year-old Shakespeare Tree and the 175-year-old, 102-foot-high Einstein Tree are both white oaks. The 150-year-old Mother Teresa Tree, a 110-foot-tall red maple, is the tallest in the grove.

■ DIRECTIONS

Take the New York Thruway (I-90) to Exit 36. Take I-81 north to Exit 28 and follow Taft Road west for 0.9 mile to Main Street. Cross Main Street and turn right onto the grounds of North Syracuse Junior High School. Park in the lot nearest the forest grove.

■ HIGHLIGHTS

Walk along the athletic field to the grove, where you'll find a single trail starting at the corner. Afterward, visit the nearby Liverpool Maple Grove, which is also owned by a school. Although the grove is only 3 acres, it includes one of the Northeast's largest forest-grown sugar maples (47 inches in diameter, 122 feet tall, 300 to 400 years old).

To get there from the Wizard of Oz Grove, head south on Route 11 and turn right on Taft Road. In a mile, turn right on Buckley Road. In about 3.6 miles, turn right on Morgan Road. In 0.75 mile, turn left on Wetzel Road. Drive 0.6 mile and turn right into Wetzel Road School parking lot. The woods are behind the lot. Explore to the left to see the giant maple.

■ CONTACT INFORMATION

North Syracuse Junior High School, 5353 West Taft Road, North Syracuse, New York 13212, 315-453-3179

42. WATKINS GLEN STATE PARK

Watkins Glen is renowned in the East for its artistically sculptured and layered chasm walls, cavernlike passageways and overhangs, and exquisite waterfalls that adorn a 3.5-mile-long gorge. But the literature never mentions that it also possesses ancient forest.

The most impressive old growth is visible from an unlabeled trail reached by a little-known side road, which travels down to a peninsula that juts into Punch Bowl Lake, 1.5 miles upstream from the entrance to Watkins Glen. Hemlock, northern red oak, white pine, and sugar maple with 36- to 45-inch trunks and ages of 150 to 300 years populate the slopes around the road. Serene Punch Bowl Lake reflects the profiles of the great trees.

■ **DIRECTIONS**

From Route 17, take Exit 52 north at Horseheads. Follow Route 14 north to the city of Watkins Glen. Park near the entrance to Watkins Glen State Park.

■ **HIGHLIGHTS**

The trail through the glen is easy to follow. Along the way, admire the waterfalls, cavelike tunnels, and mossy gorge walls. But also look for scattered small but gnarly ancient hemlocks and yellow birches growing out of the gorge walls. These bonsai-like tree forms typify the cliff-dwelling sages.

Now drive north on Route 14 for several blocks and turn left on Route 409 (Upper Glen Road). Drive up the hill and across the railroad tracks (at 1.7 miles). After another half mile, the road (now called Station Road) comes to a small grass clearing next to a short white guardrail, where you can park. The trail is on the left at a green No Hunting sign.

Walk down the woods trail from the road. You'll see impressive trees immediately. At the bottom, the trail curves to the right onto a peninsula jutting into Punch Bowl Lake.

■ **CONTACT INFORMATION**

Watkins Glen State Park, P.O. Box 304, Watkins Glen, New York 14891, 607-535-4511

43. TAUGHANNOCK FALLS STATE PARK

Thousands of people come every year to marvel at Taughannock Falls, which, at 215 feet, is one of the tallest vertical-drop waterfalls in eastern North America. As visitors gaze at the airy amphitheater of canyon wall overlooking the falls, they're bound to miss the ancient red cedars, possibly 300 or more years old, clinging to those 400-foot cliffs.

From a distance, the ancient cedars look like olive-green clumps on the cliff face, but they are actually up to 30 feet tall. Bring binoculars to get a closer look. As evergreens, these trees show up best during the cold seasons.

■ **DIRECTIONS**

From downtown Ithaca, take Route 79 west (State Street). Immediately after crossing the Cayuga Inlet, turn right on Route 89 north. Drive along the west shore of Lake Cayuga for 9 miles to the entrance to the state park, on your left. At the entrance booth, pick up a map.

First, walk the canyon bottom trail 0.75 mile to the base of the spectacular falls. The cedars are easily visible on the cliffs above. To get to the awe-inspiring canyon rim vista, continue driving north on Route 89 for 0.4 mile, take the first left onto Rice Road, and go up the hill. Turn left onto Park Road to the vista parking area on your left. Note the gnarly cedars just below the viewing overlook and on all the cliff faces.

■ CONTACT INFORMATION

New York Office of Parks and Recreation, P.O. Box 1055, Trumansburg, New York 14886, 607-387-6739

44. BEEBE LAKE WOODS, CORNELL UNIVERSITY

Cornell University has one of the country's most scenic campuses, famous for historic buildings, gardens, and cascade-graced gorges. Lesser known are its two remnants of old-growth forest, only a short distance from Cornell Plantations headquarters.

Soaring northern red and white oaks, tulip trees, and hemlocks decorate the 3-acre south slope overlooking Beebe Lake. A popular trail and Forest Home Road cut through it. A 7-acre grove overlooks the lake's northeast slope.

■ DIRECTIONS

From the junction of Routes 79 and 13 in downtown Ithaca, follow Route 79 east for about 14 blocks toward campus. After the blinking stop light, turn left on Judd Falls Road. Pass Campus Road and Morrison Hall, and turn left on

Tower Road. Drive one block to the information booth. Get directions for visitor parking, the Plantations Headquarters Building, and Forest Home Drive. Purchase the two guidebooks to natural areas on and off campus.

■ **HIGHLIGHTS**

For the best views, visit between May and October. Start by walking to the Plantations Headquarters to tour the gardens and greenhouse. Then walk along Plantations Road to Forest Home Drive. Turn left on the drive and watch for the stately trees on both sides of the road. Explore the footpaths that lead away from the road on both sides.

To visit the second grove, follow Forest Home Drive around to the east end of Beebe Lake. Watch on your left for Sackett Footbridge. Cross Fall Creek at the end of Beebe Lake. The grove is on the steep hill between the creek and the Fuertes Observatory.

Use Cornell's nature preserve guides to check out likely other old-growth forests, including Fischer Old Growth Tract, Palmer Woods, Slim Jim Woods, Fall Creek Valley, Mt. Pleasant, Renwick Slope, and Slaterville 600.

■ **CONTACT INFORMATION**

Cornell Plantations, One Plantations Road, Ithaca, New York 14850, 607-255-9638

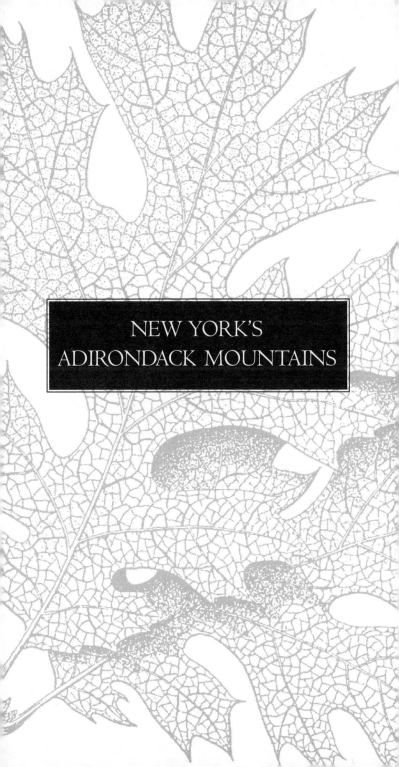

NEW YORK'S
ADIRONDACK MOUNTAINS

The Adirondacks constitute America's largest state park-land, with the greatest acreage of wilderness east of the Mississippi. At 2.8 million public acres, this preserve is larger than Yellowstone, Redwood, and Rocky Mountain National Parks combined, and it harbors 2,800 lakes, several Wild and Scenic rivers, and the Northeast's second highest mountain range. Hidden among the famed gems of this wilderness is a little-known mosaic of roughly 300,000 acres of primeval forest.

Earlier historians concluded that virtually the entire original Adirondack forest was cut, but in 1994, Barbara McMartin, author of *The Great Forest of the Adirondacks,* revealed that the state had purchased hundreds of thousands of acres before these parcels were logged or after they were very lightly logged. The actual acreage must be verified through field surveys, however. It is likely that less than 10 percent of the state lands will turn out to be big-tree old growth. Most of it may be less impressive forests of smaller old-growth trees on challenging terrain. Much may not be forest at all: open wetlands, rock outcrops, and barrens. Still other forest sites were illegally logged during earlier decades or are younger forests regenerating after storms, fires, insect damage, and acid rain. In addition, it is challenging to fit the high-elevation dwarf spruce–fir forests into the definition of old growth. Thousands of acres of these unlogged forests don't exceed 150 years of age, so they are referred to as "first growth."

Challenging bushwhacking, with expert use of maps and compass, is required to explore the vast off-trail areas, making the inventory of this great forest a worthy research project for the next aspiring great naturalist.

45. ELDERS GROVE

The colossal pines of Elders Grove form the Northeast's most impressive pine stand, matching Pennsylvania's fabulous Cook Forest. The 10-acre stand boasts a 170-foot, 60-inch-thick white pine that may be the new national champion.

Most of these rugged pines are more than 300 years old and have no limbs up to 70 feet. Their characteristics are diverse: some lean at steep angles, one has a deep lightning fissure, and the trunk of another is fused around an ancient beech. One pine twists up into the canopy like a giant serpent standing on its tail. Beneath the sky-piercing pines, other ancients include hemlock, tulip tree, red and sugar maple, black cherry, beech (unblighted!), and balsam fir (the state champion).

The grove, located on state-owned land, was discovered years ago by Dr. Michael Kudish, a botany professor at Paul Smith's College. Dr. Kudish's studies indicate the pines are near their longevity limits and are gradually dying out, with the other ancient trees taking their place.

■ **DIRECTIONS**

From Lake Placid, take Route 86 west through Saranac Lake to the junction of Route 30 at Paul Smiths hamlet. Now turn around and drive back on Route 86 a short distance. Just beyond the first 55 mph sign on the right is a steel-gated logging road. Park there, but don't block the road.

■ **HIGHLIGHTS**

Take a compass, since part of this walk is off-trail. Hike 150 yards south on the logging road to a power line. Walk 100 yards east under the power line. Just past the second power pole, hike 300 yards south on a faint forest trail with triple blazes to the old Paul Smiths box surrounding a spring. Turn east and walk 100 yards, looking for three ancient white pines in a line. Now explore the grove further.

To access nearby Cathedral Pines, a 50-acre nature preserve owned by Paul Smith's College, turn right on Route 30 from its junction with Route 86. Within 300 feet, pass Paul Smith's College entrance on the left, then make the first right and park at the back of St. Gabriel's Church lot. With your back to the church, walk to the trail on the left (red blazes). (If you see a sign-in register, you're on the wrong trail.)

Take the Red Trail straight through two trail junctions. Enter old-growth woods of hemlock, white pine, and northern hardwoods, with a narrow peninsula between two lakes.

Cross a footbridge over a channel. Bear left onto the Yellow Trail; turn left again to reach another lake. Return the way you came.

■ **CONTACT INFORMATION**
Paul Smith's College, Lands Department, Routes 86 and 30, P. O. Box 265, Paul Smiths, New York 12970, 518-327-6239

46. PINE ORCHARD

The name Pine Orchard does not convey the greatness of this forest. With colossal columns of white pine—including some reaching 145 feet and one more than 5 feet in diameter—Pine Orchard is a good place to sense what the Adirondacks looked like when only a sparse Native American population shared the forest with mountain lions, wolves, moose, and elk. This 50-acre grove also features primeval yellow birch, sugar and red maple, and impressive red spruce.

Core samplings put the pines at 185 years old, but the hemlocks and yellow birches are likely more than 300 years old. An 1815 hurricane that blew down clusters of trees left much of the virgin hemlock and northern hardwoods standing. In the small clearings of blowdown, white pines germinated. A few very old, medium-size stumps scattered about the forest are the result of illegal salvage logging following another storm in 1950.

■ **DIRECTIONS**

Take the Northway (I-87) to Exit 25 at Chestertown. Head west and south on Route 8 for 34 miles. Turn left on Route 30 south. Drive 3.7 miles and turn left on Griffin Road, after the bridge over Sacandaga River. In 0.7 mile, turn right on Windfall Road. In one mile, take the right fork at a sign for Pine Orchard, Dorr Road, Flater Road. Drive 2 miles to the end and leave your car in the visitor parking lot on the right. This is private property, so please respect the owner's hospitality.

■ **HIGHLIGHTS**

This route is 2.8 miles each way. Walk on the woods road past the house to a road gate at the state land boundary, and take the left fork. After the second brook crossing, old-growth hemlock starts on your right, then large pines appear to grow in number. At the flat top of the knoll is a small sign for Pine Orchard. Go off-trail to visit the grand pines. A dense cluster of about forty great pines populate this 120-foot knoll. Another hundred or so are visible from the trail around the knoll. On a breezy day, this is the place to listen to the mysterious sound of the wind sifting through countless pine needles.

Continue down the knoll past more colossal pines, ancient hemlocks, and yellow birches. A quarter mile farther you will reach the edge of an old beaver meadow. Our suggested route ends here. Return the way you came.

■ **CONTACT INFORMATION**

Adirondack Park Agency, P.O. Box 99, Route 86, Ray Brook, New York 12977, 518-891-4050

47. Ampersand Mountain

The primeval woods of Ampersand Mountain feature an abundance of personality: weird burls, gnarls, stilt-roots, and luxurious cushions of moss decorate the 300- to 400-year-old sugar maples and yellow birches, which reach diameters of up to 42 inches. One birch is reported to be 58 inches in diameter. Old-growth hemlock, red spruce, white pine, and beech are also scattered throughout the 2,000-acre woods.

■ **DIRECTIONS**

From Lake Placid, take Route 86 west to Saranac Lake. Five miles west of Lake Placid, you will pass Meadowbrook State Campground on your left—one of the few places where you can camp under large old-growth white pines and hemlocks (campsites 14 through 50). Turn left (west) on Route 3 and drive about 8 miles, looking on your left for the Ampersand Mountain trail sign and parking area on the right.

■ **HIGHLIGHTS**

Walk across the road and pass the metal gate onto the trail, where the primeval forest begins. Make sure to examine the mossy majesty of the trees, with their burls, buttresses, and stilt-roots. The first 1.5 miles through the big-tree forest are relatively flat. When the trail starts its steep ascent, you can turn back or make the 1,900-foot, 1.3-mile climb up Ampersand Mountain (3,352-foot elevation) for an awesome panoramic view.

■ **CONTACT INFORMATION**

Adirondack Park Agency, P.O. Box 99, Route 86, Ray Brook, New York 12977, 518-891-4050

48. Pack Forest

A charming cathedral of noble white pines and hemlocks enchant the visitor to the 47-acre Charles Lathrop Pack Forest. With nine white pines between 120 and 147 feet tall and exceeding 42 inches in diameter, this forest will remind you of the Pacific Northwest. The Grandmother's Tree, a 300-year-old white pine, is 52.7 inches in diameter and an impressive 147.2 feet tall. While not as impressive in height, the hemlocks are the oldest, typically 250 to 280 years old. A large red spruce on the right near the trail's beginning is 100.3 feet tall and 30 inches in diameter, impressive for this species. Other senior citizens include yellow birch, red maple, and sugar maple.

Pack Forest was donated to the state by Charles Pack, an early timber company owner known for logging thousands of acres in the Adirondacks. This ancient forest, however, was next to his home, and when his wife learned of his plans to cut the magnificent trees, she threatened to never cook another meal for him. His stomach won out.

■ **DIRECTIONS**

From the Northway (I-87), take Exit 23 at Warrensburg. Head west into Warrensburg on Route 9 north. In 2.8 miles, at the junction with Route 28, veer right on Route 9. Follow it for 0.3 mile to the Pack Forest entrance on your left. Drive past the main house to the parking area, where the nature trail starts.

■ **HIGHLIGHTS**

This forest is special because of its wheelchair-accessible 1.5-mile nature trail. You immediately enter big timber, with large pines forming an impressive corridor to the left. After passing through ancient hemlocks, the trail reaches the second area of big pines, including the Grandmother Tree. The trail brochure lists it as "175 feet high, the tallest in the state." Our careful measurements show that this number was overestimated by 28 feet. The trail loops back to your car past mirrorlike ponds.

- **CONTACT INFORMATION**

State University of New York College of Environmental Science and Forestry, P.O. Box 158, Warrensburg, New York 12885, 518-623-9679

49. WILCOX MOUNTAIN

New York's most impressive array of primeval sugar maples covers a 1,000-acre area on Wilcox Mountain near Warrensburg. Each of the 300- to 400-year-old sugar maples, which reach 4 feet in diameter, stands out with unique knots, burls, cavities, and fissures. Other aged specimens exhibiting equal character include yellow birch, hemlock, white pine, and white ash.

On the day of our visit, the forest was in fog, and each tree column cast a silhouette that conveyed a primal and mysterious aura.

- **DIRECTIONS**

From the Northway (I-87), take Exit 23 west into Warrensburg on Route 9 north. From downtown Warrensburg, turn left on Route 418. Go 3.5 miles and cross the Hudson River. Immediately turn left on River Road-Warrensburg

Road, which parallels the river. Set your odometer. In 9 miles, enter Stoney Creek hamlet and turn right on Harrisburg Road. Drive north and west 10.7 miles, passing Harrisburg Lake Lodge. The pavement becomes a dirt road and gets rougher. Park off the road before the creek ford.

■ **HIGHLIGHTS**

Cross the creek on the snowmobile bridge and pass the private Moosewood Club. The road becomes more rutted and potholed. Avoid wet periods because of mud and flooding. In 1.2 miles, turn right across the suspension bridge over Stoney Creek. The trail climbs up for a half mile.

Turn left on the trail at the top. On the gentle climb up Wilcox Mountain, you enter an inspiring, mile-long gallery of great maples. Venture off-trail to examine more trees, then return to the trail and gradually descend past several splendid pines at pristine Wilcox Brook. The old growth becomes spotty on the next 1.5 miles of trail, but the scenery is worth the walk. Return the way you came.

■ **CONTACT INFORMATION**

Adirondack Park Agency, P.O. Box 99, Route 86, Ray Brook, New York 12977, 518-891-4050

50. ADIRONDACK MOUNTAIN RESERVE

Nestled within the Adirondacks' spectacular Ausable Lakes Gorge are 1,150 acres of primeval big-tree forest on the lands of the private Adirondack Mountain Reserve.

Majestic stands of hemlock, yellow birch, and sugar maple

adorn miles of footpaths that are open to the public. Primitive hemlock more than 4 feet thick, 100 feet high, and 300 years old command attention on the trails. Patriarchal yellow birches and shaggy sugar maples display their own rustic elegance. Smaller virgin forests and subalpine and alpine communities cover the upper slopes around the big trees.

The reserve also offers scenes straight out of the Canadian Rockies. Waterfalls trip down cliffs. Mossy chutes and crystalline pools create a magical atmosphere. Jaw-dropping, jagged cliffs of twenty "high peaks," with elevations of more than 4,000 feet, command the heights over the 2,100-foot gorge.

■ DIRECTIONS

Take the Northway (I-87) to the exit for Route 73-Lake Placid. Drive 7.3 miles north on Route 73. Turn left and drive on the little road to the parking area. Note: on popular weekends, the lot fills up, so arrive before 10:30 a.m.

■ HIGHLIGHTS

Walk 0.9 mile up the road past the golf course. Near Ausable Club Lodge, turn left past a tennis court to the entrance gate at the woods road. Pick up a map and pay the fee.

In 1.8 miles, turn left on Gill Brook Trail to see primeval forest, ancient cedars hanging on cliffs, and the sublime pools of Artist's Falls. At 1.3 miles (a 500-foot ascent), watch for the Bypass Trail, which angles back to your right.

Take the next right off Gill Brook Trail to continue up 500 feet to spectacular views at Indian Head. From there, take the first right-hand trail steeply down to the valley and the lake. For a less strenuous hike, return to the Bypass Trail. When you reach the dirt road, turn left for the lake vista.

From the lake, head back along the road. Look for the trail on the left to Rainbow Falls. Cross Ausable River bridge and follow the sign to Rainbow Falls, not up the mountain. The awesome, 150-foot ribbon falls is one of the finest in the Northeast.

Return toward the river, but don't cross it. Turn left on the West River Trail to reenter ancient forest. In 1 mile, turn right. Cross Ausable River, then turn left on East River Trail. In a minute, turn right, head away from the river, and go past more forest veterans. At the dirt road, turn left. In 1.9 miles, pass the entrance booth. Turn right near the hotel and return to your car.

- **CONTACT INFORMATION**

Adirondack Park Agency, P.O. Box 99, Route 86, Ray Brook, New York 12977, 518-891-4050

51. FIVE PONDS WILDERNESS

The Northeast's largest protected wilderness, the 95,525-acre Five Ponds, also possesses the region's largest un-logged tract—some 50,000 acres. Only three trails partially pierce the forbiddingly wild landscape, which harbors ninety-five ponds, two state Wild Rivers, and fifty hills up to 700 feet high.

Tragically, the great storm of 1995 blew down 10,000 acres of old growth, but clusters of grand old trees still stand along some stretches of trail. Elsewhere, most of the big trees now lie on the ground. The surviving big white pine, hemlock, yellow birch, and sugar maple reach diameters of 3 to

4.5 feet and ages of 250 to 400 years. Red spruce, usually modestly sized trees, attain notable diameters of 22 inches.

■ **DIRECTIONS**

From Lake Placid, take Route 86 west to Saranac Lake, then Route 3 west past Tupper Lake to Cranberry Lake. From the village of Cranberry Lake, continue west on Route 3 for 7.6 miles and turn south on the road to Wanakena. After 1 mile, bear right. Make a second right and cross a little bridge over Oswegatchie River. Drive 0.6 mile along South Shore Road to the parking area.

■ **HIGHLIGHTS**

Before starting, contact the forest ranger for updated trail information. The trail starts on the south side of the road. Take the High Falls Loop Trail southeast for 3.6 miles to the end of Dead Creek Flow. At Cat Mountain Trail, turn left and go 1.25 miles. Pass pockets of old growth, and reach the summit for a vista of the blowdown area. Return from here.

If you are backpacking, continue south on High Falls Loop Trail through blowdown. Turn left at a trail, go 0.4 mile to Oswegatchie River to see High Falls. Return to the trail junction and turn left (south). In 1.1 miles, turn left on the blue Five Ponds Trail. Cross the river. In 1.5 miles, you'll see the old-growth survivors, which continue for the next mile. Explore the primeval forest along Big Shallow Pond, Big Five Pond, and the esker ridges. Camp overnight in lean-tos.

■ **CONTACT INFORMATION**

Adirondack Park Agency, P.O. Box 99, Route 86, Ray Brook, New York 12977, 518-891-4050. Ask for the number for the forest ranger for that district.

52. ROARING BROOK FALLS

A popular scenic site since the 1800s, Roaring Brook Falls plunges 200 feet in two steps down the southeast flank of 4,000-foot Giant Mountain, the state's tallest peak when measured from base to summit. A 170-acre ancient forest fills the falls' valley and the steep slopes around it.

Roaring Brook's ancient forest is special because the tree ages are easy to determine here. Two hemlocks, which fell across the trail in 1995, were cut to expose their annual rings. One log cut 15 feet from its base has 425 years of rings, which means its age could be up to 475 years. Other hemlocks nearby are larger and could be older.

Although the trees are only moderately sized, they are ancient. The largest hemlock we have seen is 38 inches in diameter. Yellow birch, sugar maple, white ash, and red oak have diameters of 24 to 36 inches. The lowest boughs of some maple and ash start as high as 65 feet.

■ DIRECTIONS

Take I-87 (Northway) to the exit for Route 73-Lake Placid. Drive 7.4 miles, watching carefully on your right for the small dirt pull-off. If you come to a sign for St. Huberts, you passed the pull-off.

■ HIGHLIGHTS

On the trail, you enter old growth within 500 feet, where a maple towers over you on the left. At the fork, take the right trail. Watch for the cut log so you can count its rings. Just ahead is the falls. The lower falls ricochet down the vertical slot in the cliff. At low water, you can climb over rocks to its bottom. Do not try to climb the cliff—it's slick and dangerous.

Return to the trail fork and turn right, up the hill. Watch as the trees get larger. Partway up, at the first terrace, walk off the main trail along a smaller path that follows the edge of the slope. You will walk past even larger specimens. The path reconnects with the main trail to the left. Follow it up to where you can see the upper falls.

■ **CONTACT INFORMATION**

Adirondack Park Agency, P.O. Box 99, Route 86, Ray Brook, New York 12977, 518-891-4050

53. High Falls Gorge and White Face Mountain

Ancient trees line the trail, cling to the cliff, and perch on the ledges of High Falls Gorge, a stupendous series of torrential cataracts and chasms on the Ausable River. This is one Adirondack sight you must not miss. Nearly all the trees are hemlocks or northern white cedars between 200 and 500 years old.

■ **DIRECTIONS AND HIGHLIGHTS**

From Lake Placid Village, take Route 86 north. Enter the spectacular, 1,700-foot gorge of Wilmington Notch, whose cliff faces and ledges are covered with ancient, gnarled conifers. High Falls Gorge is just ahead on your left. Take your time along the paths and boardwalks to appreciate the waterfalls and the bizarrely shaped primeval trees.

After High Falls Gorge, drive north on Route 86. Turn left at signs to Whiteface Mountain Scenic Road, the second highest road in the Northeast. It takes you almost to the top of 4,865-foot Whiteface Mountain. Along the way, you'll pass through a dwarf forest of virgin subalpine spruce and fir. Famous for its role in the Olympic games, the peak offers a matchless panorama and is the state's only alpine tundra reachable by car. Some of the crusty patches of colorful lichens are many centuries old.

- **CONTACT INFORMATION**

Roanka Attractions (High Falls Gorge), Route 86 at Wilmington Notch, Wilmington, New York 12997, 518-946-2278

54. St. Regis Canoe Area

Aisles of centuries-old soaring pines line the fifty-eight ponds and esker ridges of the St. Regis Canoe Area, creating scenes that resemble classic paintings. The 26,880-acre property near Saranac Lake has been one of the premier canoe paradises in the Northeast since the 1880s.

- **DIRECTIONS**

From Lake Placid, take Route 86 west past Saranac Lake to Route 30. Head south on Route 30 for 2.5 miles. At 0.35 mile past the state fish hatchery, turn right (north) onto a dirt road. Immediately after the railroad tracks, take the right fork, which leads to the canoe landing on Little Clear Pond.

- **HIGHLIGHTS**

Obtain a canoe map to follow this 3.6-mile out-and-back route. Paddle to the northwest end of Little Clear Pond. Notice the old "flag" pines along the shore that point leeward from the wind. At the north end, land your canoe toward the left (northwest) end. A 0.3-mile portage brings you to St. Regis Pond, ringed by more ancient conifer trees.

Steer leftward toward the northwest corner of St. Regis Pond to spy the next canoe carry trail. It takes you a half mile to little Ochre Pond, with more primeval scenery. Aim for the northwest corner of this pond. In 0.6 mile, the portage trail comes to within sight of the narrow sliver called Mud Pond. Stay high on the ridge so you don't miss the aisle of enormous pines. About 0.4 mile further, you arrive at Fish Pond, also ringed by glorious forest.

Canoe to the southwest end and you have a very short canoe portage to Little Long Pond. Return the way you came or use a map to extend your trip to many more lakes.

■ **CONTACT INFORMATION**

Saranac Chamber of Commerce (for the nearest canoe rentals), 30 Main Street, Saranac Lake, New York 12983, 800-347-1992

55. GOLDMINE CREEK

Stepping onto the Goldmine Creek Trail is like stepping back in time. You are immediately surrounded by a wild, dense forest of strangely shaped trees, cloaked with garlands of ferns and gowns of moss. The trail is narrow and rarely traveled and is surrounded by 2,000 acres of old-growth forest that is still largely unexplored.

Many large yellow birches and hemlocks reach 400 to 450 years old. One yellow birch measures an astonishing 54 inches in diameter, but most are 34 to 42 inches thick. These crusty old critters have character. One colossal yellow birch has a 6-foot-wide burl, a massive virus-caused swelling, projecting from its trunk. Champion 300-year-old red spruce have trunks 32 inches thick and stand 106 feet tall. At this latitude, this species is usually not more than 15 to 20 inches thick. The flaky bark sometimes displays an indescribable purple hue. Ancient sugar and red maples and black cherry also thrive here.

Goldmine Creek got its name from a legend that it was near a gold mine. However, gold deposits have never been recorded in New York State.

■ **DIRECTIONS**

Take the New York Thruway (Route 90) to Exit 31. Follow Route 8 north for 54 miles past Piseco Lake. Turn right (south) on Route 10. Drive exactly 1.2 miles and turn right on the gravel Powley Road just after a bridge over a stream.

Now set your odometer. The first several miles are through younger and mature forest. At 4.9 miles, you will enter the old growth between East and West Notch Mountains. Stop and walk over to the ancient trees on the rock ledges of the notch. In 0.5 mile, you'll drive out of the narrowest part of the notch. Along this road, we measured some of the East Coast's largest red spruce, reaching more than 31 inches in diameter and 105 feet in height.

At about 6.3 miles, carefully watch for a small, open grassy area on your left. Park here so you won't pass the nearly invisible trail entrance.

■ **HIGHLIGHTS**

This is wild country, so carry a compass and a map. Walking along the right side of the road, head 30 feet past the south edge of the meadow and look carefully on your right for an obscure trail. The path's beginning is marked by three slashes in a tree that were painted black by vandals.

Walk only 120 feet to where you see two overturned trees on your left, next to the trail. Peer into the forest to see a giant birch, 150 feet into the woods on your left. Walk off the trail to admire one of the largest birches, and one of the largest birch burls, in the eastern United States.

Back on the 1.3-mile trail, take caution on the slippery, round wood steps across wet areas. Watch carefully on your left for an unmarked, and misleading, side trail. Bear right at this junction (memorize this spot so you won't take the wrong trail back). Almost a mile from the road, you'll come to a stream that may be flooded by a beaver dam. If so, cut to the left into the woods to find a downstream spot you can cross, then return to the trail on the other side.

Ten minutes later, you'll hear the rushing of Goldmine Creek on your left. Leave the main trail so you can walk along the creek, with its primordial scene of waterfalls and chutes. But remember this spot so you don't pass it on your way back and miss the trail. Don't miss the deep cleft with cascades.

Return the same way you came (east on your compass). Remember to bear left at the tricky side trail ahead.

■ **CONTACT INFORMATION**

Adirondack Park Agency, P.O. Box 99, Route 86, Ray Brook, New York 12977, 518-891-4050

56. Panther Mountain and Piseco Lake

The Northeast's largest birch trees, as well as an impressive array of other large trees, grow in the 6,000-acre swath of ancient forest that extends from Fawn Lake southwest to Panther Mountain, overlooking Piseco Lake. It is part of an even larger zone, barely explored, spanning much of the West Canada Lakes Wilderness to the north.

The Chief Jake Swamp Tree, a champion yellow birch 57.3 inches in diameter and 95.5 feet tall, grows along a feeder stream near Little Sand Point State Campground on Piseco Lake's west shore. Other champion yellow birches grow in the area along with red spruce (up to 27 inches thick, 100 feet tall, and 265 years old), hemlocks (up to 39 inches in diameter), and a tall, straight hop hornbeam with an incredible 25-inch diameter. The white ash, sugar maple, and basswood are impressive, too.

- **DIRECTIONS**

Take New York Thruway (Route 90) to Exit 31. Follow Route 8 north for 51 miles. Turn left onto West Shore Piseco Road, marked by signs for Point Comfort and Little Sand Point campgrounds. (If you reach the shore of Piseco Lake or Route 10, you passed the turnoff.) Drive 2.6 miles on West Shore Piseco Road and park at the pull-off on the right, opposite the trailhead for Echo Cliff Trail.

- **HIGHLIGHTS**

This steep 0.75-mile trail ascends Panther Mountain. After the first quarter mile, the trail is lined with old-growth forest, including the massive yellow birches. Your second re-

ward is Echo Cliff, 700 feet above the lake, which offers terrific views across Spy Lake to the Silver Lake Wilderness,
another primeval forest area. The summit of Panther Mountain is covered by a thicket of dwarf old-growth balsam fir.

■ **CONTACT INFORMATION**

Adirondack Park Agency, P.O. Box 99, Route 86, Ray
Brook, New York 12977, 518-891-4050

57. RAQUETTE LAKE RED PINES

Glowing bright orange in the late afternoon sun, this 10-
acre stand of rare red pines at Raquette Lake is stunning to
behold. In the Northeast, these trees come closest to repli-
cating the West's famous ponderosa pines, which also have
orange bark, though with much larger rectangular plates.

These red pines grow to 28 inches in diameter, 115 feet
in height, and 200 or more years in age. Among them are
even larger white pines, some 42 inches in diameter. All
grow on a southward-facing slope, overlooking the South
Inlet of Raquette Lake.

■ **DIRECTIONS**

At the hamlet of Blue Mountain Lake where Routes 28 and
30 meet, go west on Route 28 for 10.2 miles. Just before the
bridge across the South Inlet of Raquette Lake, park in the
dirt pull-off on the left.

■ **HIGHLIGHTS**

Time your visit for a sunny afternoon. Walk toward the
bridge and turn left on a short path that climbs the little knoll

to the red pines. Stay on the high path, and go off-trail to the left to see the impressive white pines on the top of the knoll. Then sample the low path and the rest of the red pines.

■ **CONTACT INFORMATION**

Adirondack Park Agency, P.O. Box 99, Route 86, Ray Brook, New York 12977, 518-891-4050

58. CATHEDRAL PINES OF SEVENTH LAKE

With huge white pines around 200 years old, the 3-acre Cathedral Pines grove is the perfect introduction to old growth for people who want a quick and easy look at these masterpieces. This site, near Seventh Lake, one of the Fulton Chain of Lakes, lies only 100 feet from the road.

This protected area contains one of the Adirondacks' tallest white pines—152.1 feet tall and 41.8 inches in diameter—as well as ten trees that are 40 inches or more in diameter.

■ **DIRECTIONS AND HIGHLIGHTS**

At the intersection of Route 28 and Route 30, drive west 17.2 miles on Route 28 to the Eighth Lake Campground entrance sign, on your right. In another 0.8 mile, look on your right for a brown wooden trail sign marking the Cathedral Pines. (It is also 1 mile north of the Seventh Lake fishing access sign.) The loop trail is only an eighth of a mile long.

■ **CONTACT INFORMATION**

Adirondack Park Agency, P.O. Box 99, Route 86, Ray Brook, New York 12977, 518-891-4050

59. Shelving Rock

Classic scenes out of a Romantic Era painting await you at Shelving Rock, a jagged protrusion created by a cliffy dome, 800 feet over Lake George. Indeed, Lake George and the Tongue Mountain Range appear in old paintings now displayed in museums. But with sublime lake vistas and an ancient forest that begins right at the parking lot, the real thing is even better.

Due to early and sporadic selective logging, the large trees are distributed irregularly along the route. Surrounding the first section is a grove of monumental 300-year-old hemlocks and white pines. Another ancient section of hemlock, black birch, and sugar maple starts on the top of the ridge, and continues down the ravine. Massive specimens of northern white cedar, an old-growth rarity, cling to ledges. Along the lakeshore, the wonderful carriage road passes by beautiful mature forest and clusters of ancient hemlock, cedar, red oak, and maple.

Prior to World War I, when the state acquired it, Shelving Rock was a nineteenth-century tourist hotel retreat. Walking along the hotel road, you can visualize horse-drawn carriages with Victorian ladies in long gowns and formally dressed men in top hats.

■ **DIRECTIONS**

From the Northway (I-87), just south of Lake George, take Exit 20. Go north on Route 9, then take Route 149 for 5.4 miles east. Turn left on Buttermilk Falls Road and set your odometer. The road soon turns left and becomes Sly Pond Road, then Shelving Rock Road. Follow it north for 12.1 miles, then park on your right under the huge hemlocks. Before you walk on the trail, visit the sentinel hemlocks on the other side of the road.

■ **HIGHLIGHTS**

Head up the ravine on the yellow-marked trail for 10 minutes through serene ancient forest, and you'll reach a trail on your left. In 20 minutes, leave old growth and climb 350 feet to the top of the ridge and a trail junction.

Turn right and pass scattered ancient trees for the next 10 minutes. The next left-hand trail descends 560 feet through a wild ravine of hulking hemlocks. Walk to the bottom of the ledges on your right to look up at champion-size white cedars that may exceed 600 years in age.

When you get to the bottom, you are on the old hotel carriage road. Take the right-hand stretch. Scattered old-growth trees decorate the woods in between stretches of mature second-growth woods.

About a half mile along the lane, scoot down to the shore to a rocky point and a little bay for an enchanting lake vista of pretty islands and the 2,000-foot Tongue Mountains, across to the right. Walk on the lake road as far as you wish. Return the same way.

■ **CONTACT INFORMATION**

Adirondack Park Agency, P.O. Box 99, Route 86, Ray Brook, New York 12977, 518-891-4050

HUDSON RIVER VALLEY
and
NEW YORK METRO AREA

Because of their easy access from the coast and up the Hudson River, the Hudson River Valley and the New York metro area were settled between the 1600s and early 1700s—long before the rest of the state. This means that the forests in these regions have endured a long period of time in which to be cut, cleared, and burned. Nonetheless, a surprising amount of old growth has survived, thanks to the foresight of early landowners and the remote locations of some forests.

Since the late 1600s, Long Island, New York City, and the Hudson River corridor have been choice locations for large estates. Many estate owners protected their original forests, which have since become public parks or preserves. A number of these ancient forests are within New York City, including Manhattan's Inwood Hill Park.

To the north of the city, forests along the steep terrain and cliffs were sequestered from the ravages of development.

The Shawangunk Ridge and the Catskill Mountains, which harbor considerable old growth, were spared in this way. Indeed, 65,000 acres of subalpine dwarf old-growth forests blanket the summits of the Catskill Mountains. (Unfortunately, we know relatively little about big-tree old growth on the lower slopes.) This region inspired the famous nineteenth-century Hudson River School of landscape painting that included Romantic Era painters such as Thomas Cole who often included virgin forests in their work. Cole's renowned painting of Kaaterskill Falls and its primeval trees represents the site just as realistically today as it did then.

In southern New York, several sites deserve special mention because, until the 1980s, most authorities believed there were only two old-growth groves in this region: the New York Botanical Garden Forest in the Bronx and the Mianus River Gorge, 30 miles north of New York City. The Mianus River Gorge was the first preserve of the Nature Conservancy.

Since the 1980s, however, experts have documented nearly three dozen sites in this region. Among them are several major surprises, including a dozen old-growth groves that have survived within New York's five boroughs and a number on or near Long Island. The 3,500-acre Gardiners Island, off the eastern tip of Long Island, harbors 400 or more acres of ancient maritime oak forest—the largest big-tree old-growth forest in the region. Just a mile from Long Island's easternmost tip at Montauk Point is a unique upland moss-covered forest of towering 300-year-old black gums with ancient hollies and oaks.

Today, the area surrounding the Hudson River Valley remains one of the least explored parts of New York State, but that is likely to change with the recently formed Eastern New

York Old-Growth Forest Survey Team. Among its major discoveries are two of the state's oldest tree communities, the
dwarf red cedars on the cliffs of Vroman's Nose, which are
more than 600 years old, and the rugged Palmaghatt Ravine
ancient forest, with its 500-year-old hemlocks.

Unfortunately, the Hudson River Valley and New York
metro area were the first regions to become infested by the
hemlock adelgid insect. This became an epidemic that has
killed nearly all coastal zone mature and old-growth hemlocks from Rhode Island to New Jersey. Tragically, it is con-
tinuing to spread to the north, south, and west, and treatment
is effective only in small, select areas; it is prohibitively ex-
pensive in larger regions.

60. MOHONK MOUNTAIN AND PRESERVE

Lining the Catskill Mountains' southern edge, the 25,000-
acre Shawangunk Mountain ridge boasts sweeping vistas,
two dozen waterfalls, stunning mountaintop lakes, and a
world-class lodge built in 1869. Shawangunk's 400-foot
cliffs are the East Coast's most popular rock-climbing site.

Despite this area's popularity, its ancient trees are largely
unrecognized. It has the state's most primeval forest outside
the Adirondacks, including 400- to 550-year-old hemlocks
that reach 45 inches in diameter. Nearly as old yellow and
black birch, 300-year-old pitch pine, and red cedar are an
artist's delight. The 2,200-acre Mohonk Mountain House
tract and adjacent 6,300-acre Mohonk Preserve feature un-
forgettable routes with ladders, wooden walkways, and steps

that take you through rock crevices, around jagged boulders, and along cliff-top ledges covered with these ancient trees.

■ DIRECTIONS

From the New York Thruway (Route 87), take Exit 18. Turn west on Route 299 and go through New Paltz, where you can purchase a trail guide. When Route 299 leaves New Paltz and crosses the Wallkill River bridge, turn right. Drive 4 miles on Mountain Rest Road, following signs to Mohonk Mountain House. The entrance is on your left. Arrive by 10 a.m. on summer weekends before the lot fills up.

■ HIGHLIGHTS

Bring sturdy boots, water, food, a camera, and binoculars for this strenuous hike. At the gate house, get a trail map and directions for the shuttle bus. Pay the day-use fee and take the shuttle bus up to the Picnic Lodge. Walk a quarter mile to Mohonk Lake and follow the sign to the greenhouse, the lake, and Skytop. Turn left at Huguenot Drive to see exquisite Mohonk Gardens on the left. Once you reach the hotel and Mohonk Lake, turn left and look for the Labyrinth Trail on your left.

The hour-long Labyrinth Trail is a demanding crevice-and-rock scramble adventure with ladders. Near the start, note the 500-year-old hemlock growing up from the bottom of a 40-foot-deep crevice. At the top of the crevice, walk to the end of the rock platform to see a hundred ancient "daredevil" pines clinging to the cliff.

Follow the trail up to Skytop Road for a panorama of six states. From the tower, head toward the cliff, but turn right on the road. Take Skytop Path to the lakeshore and turn left on Lakeshore Road. Halfway along the lake, turn right onto Lake Shore Path.

Take the Lake Shore Path past the end of the lake and turn right on Short Woodland Drive. Then turn right on Humpty Dumpty Road. After Copes Lookout, turn left on the blue Cathedral Path, which drops steeply through boulders and ancient rock-dwelling trees. Turn left on the red Arching Rocks Path to see 4-foot-diameter hemlocks and white pines. Turn right on Giants Path, then left onto Giants Workshop Path, another challenging scramble past ancient trees.

Descend to Laurel Ledge Road and turn right. In a mile, at a very sharp angle to the right, look for the blue Maple Path on the left. Soon, turn left on the Stokes Trail and right again on a side trail that ends at Mossy Brook Road. Turn left here, then turn right on Cedar Drive and right again onto Rock Rift Road. In 500 feet, look carefully on your left for the red-blazed Rock Rift Path.

Explore the passages of cavelike Rock Rift. Among the ancient trees you'll find are a huge yellow birch, with a 120-foot-long network of cablelike surface roots, wedged into the crevice.

Exit the Rifts, turn right on Old Glen Anna Road and pass through mature forest with some old-growth hemlocks. At the next woods road, turn right. Turn left at the next road and left again on Whitney Road. Turn left at Huguenot Path and take this to the parking lot.

■ **CONTACT INFORMATION**

Mohonk Preserve, 1000 Mountain Rest Road, New Paltz, New York 12561, 914-255-0919

61. Minnewaska State Park

Just a short distance from Mohonk, 12,000-acre Minnewaska State Park and its adjacent 4,600-acre nonprofit land trust feature some of the same ancient tree views but without the difficult scrambles on ladders and along ledges.

▪ DIRECTIONS

Follow the previous directions to New Paltz, then take Route 299 west. Turn right on Route 44/55, which steeply winds up Trapps Ridge, the East Coast's most popular climbing area. At the top of the ridge, drive 3 more miles. Turn left at the Minnewaska Park entrance. Get a map and drive up to the highest parking lot. On popular weekends, arrive by 10 a.m. or the parking lot will be filled.

▪ HIGHLIGHTS

Walk up the road to the cliff panorama over Minnewaska Lake. Note the many ancient pines and hemlocks on the cliffs around the lake. Follow the road to your right. Now use your trail map to reach three more old-growth sites. Head to the green-blazed Awosting Lake Road, and follow it 3 miles to the blue-blazed Long Path on your right. This quickly takes you into an old-growth hemlock forest and the 75-foot-high Rainbow Falls.

Return to Awosting Road and head west to Lake Awosting and its spectacular cliffs. Then take a southwest trail to the yellow-blazed Hamilton Point Road, which follows dramatic cliffs to Hamilton Point and Echo Rock. Isolated ancient pitch pines cling to all the cliffs. Peer into the wild Palmaghatt Ravine, where groves of huge 500-year-old hemlocks grow in the abyss below. When the yellow-blazed trail meets the red trail overlooking Minnewaska Lake, turn left and return to your car.

■ **CONTACT INFORMATION**
Palisades Interstate Park Commission, P.O. Box 893, New Paltz, New York 12561, 914-255-0919

62. KAATERSKILL CLOVE AND KAATERSKILL FALLS

Visiting Kaaterskill Falls is like stepping into a classic Romantic Era painting. The 260-foot-high waterfall is one of the most well known images from the Hudson River School of landscape painting, and some of Kaaterskill's ancient trees may be the same ones shown in the famous nineteenth-century painting.

The falls and the ancient forest haven't changed much since those days. On the great cliffs at the falls, craggy trees wrap their roots around boulders, which has enabled these trees to stay upright for centuries. Despite very shallow soils, the 250- to 400-year-old virgin hemlocks reach 44 inches in diameter and 110 feet in height. The gorge's tallest tree is a 113.7-foot white ash across Lake Creek.

■ **DIRECTIONS**
Take Route 87 (New York Thruway) to Exit 21 at Catskill. Drive east on Route 23, then south on Route 9W. Turn right on Route 23A and follow it 7 miles into Palenville. When it meets Route 32A, take Route 23A west for 3.5 miles. The public parking area is at a sharp bend in the road.

■ **HIGHLIGHTS**

To get to the trail, walk downhill (east) along the road to the trailhead on your left. Although the 0.4-mile trail parallels the creek, walk along the creek shore once you are above the 85-foot Lower Falls. At the base of the 175-foot Upper Falls, spy the lone sentinel pine (98 feet tall and as old as 275 years) leaning over the left side of the falls. The official trail to the top of the falls was closed because of accidents, so scramble to the top at your own risk.

After this hike, you can observe 250 acres of old growth while driving through nearby rugged Stony Clove Notch. Drive 6 miles west on Route 23A. Turn left on Route 214, which goes through the notch. At Devil's Path Campground, you can also hike on Devil's Path to the top of Plateau Mountain to see dwarf ancient birch and spruce forest. The trail starts at the south end of Notch Lake, crosses Route 214 and steeply climbs 1,650 feet. The elfin, moss-carpeted forest covers the flat 3,840-foot-high summit.

■ **CONTACT INFORMATION**

New York Department of Environmental Conservation, Region 3 Office, 21 South Putt Corners Road, New Paltz, New York 12561, 914-255-5453

63. MT. WITTENBURG AND CORNELL MOUNTAIN

At 4,180 feet, Slide Mountain and its neighbors, including Mt. Wittenburg and Cornell Mountain, constitute the highest range in the Catskills. They are cloaked in nearly 16,000 acres of ancient dwarf forest comprising red spruce, balsam fir, and yellow birch at the upper latitudes, and beech and hemlock below 3,000 feet.

■ DIRECTIONS

Take New York Thruway (Route 87) to Exit 19 at Kingston. Follow Route 28 west 25 miles to Route 214 at Phoenicia. Turn right on Route 214, then immediate left onto High Street, which goes under the Route 28 overpass. In 1 mile, turn left on Woodland Valley Road. Drive 4.7 miles and enter Woodland Valley Campground. The hikers' parking lot is ahead on the right.

■ HIGHLIGHTS

Cross the road to the red Wittenburg-Slide Mountain Trail. The 2,400-foot climb to Mt. Wittenburg and Cornell Mountain is 9.4 miles round trip. The first 1,000 feet are very steep and lead you through a big-tree virgin forest of hemlock and sugar maple.

After a mile, turn right at a trail junction to stay on the red trail, which steepens again. Within an hour, you reach Mt. Wittenburg's summit. The vista to the east is terrific. On the way to Cornell Mountain, the ancient red spruce get much larger between the peaks. At the top, walk 500 feet to a lookout to see Slide Mountain. Also take a short trail to the left to Cornell's summit. Return the way you came.

■ CONTACT INFORMATION

New York Department of Environmental Conservation, Region 3 Office, 21 South Putt Corners Road, New Paltz, New York 12561, 914-255-5453

64. Giant Ledge and Panther Mountain

Although the 300-foot walls of Giant Ledge are enormous, the forest at its summit is elfin. Because of the severe climate, these dwarf black cherry trees are small in size but large in character, with gnarly, twisted, contorted shapes. Massive old-growth trees here reside at the bottom of Giant Ledge. Red spruce grow to 31 inches in diameter and hemlocks to 39 inches in this trailless area. Other ancient trees include yellow birch and northern red oak.

■ **DIRECTIONS**

Take New York Thruway (Route 87) to Exit 19 at Kingston. Follow Route 28 west for 31 miles to Big Indian. Turn left on Route 47. Drive south 7.3 miles uphill to the hairpin turn where the large parking area is on your right.

■ **HIGHLIGHTS**

Walk up the road 200 feet to the yellow Phoenicia-East Branch Trail on your left. It is 1.6 miles and a 1,000-foot climb to Giant Ledge. After a half mile, at a ledge area, notice the large scattered sugar maples, up to 44 inches in diameter, and shaggy hemlock groves just off-trail.

On the ridge line, turn left (north) on the Blue Trail, where you'll see some gnarly trees. Take paths to the right to lookouts over the big-tree old growth below and the fabulous panorama of the Catskills' highest peaks. Return the way you came.

New York Department of Environmental Conservation, Region 3 Office, 21 South Putt Corners Road, New Paltz, New York 12561, 914-255-5453

65. LISHA KILL NATURAL AREA

Lisha Kill Natural Area, purchased by the Nature Conservancy in 1964, is one of the few original forests in the Mohawk River Valley. About 30 acres of the nature preserve's 108 acres are old-growth hemlock, white pine, northern red and white oak, and beech. Nearly vertical walls of Lisha Kill's gorge accent the trees' tall trunks that grow up to 42 inches thick. The trees form a canopy over the forest floor, which is largely free of plant growth because so little light penetrates. Gurgling water echoes in the mossy gorge.

■ DIRECTIONS

Take Route 87 (Northway) north to Exit 6 (Latham). Turn left on Route 7, go 4.5 miles, then turn right on Mohawk Road. In less than a mile, turn left at a T-junction, onto Rosendale Road. In a mile, pass Lock 7 Road. When you pass River Road, drive another 0.2 mile and watch carefully for an old building, formerly a firehouse, and a grange hall on your left. Park between the two.

■ HIGHLIGHTS

Walk between the buildings to the back. The 1.5-mile red trail loop enters the old forest after a trail box. Pass under beautiful hemlocks, white pines, and oaks to an overlook of the Fly Kill's gorge. Then bear left and follow the edge of the Lisha Kill gorge. After several bends of the gorge, the trail loops back through the old woods. When it rejoins the original trail, turn right and return to your car.

The preserve is closed late February to early May.

■ CONTACT INFORMATION

The Nature Conservancy, 19 North Moger Avenue, Mt. Kisco, New York 10549, 914-244-3271

66. OLD MAIDS WOODS

With dark, deeply corrugated bark armoring their massive columns, the black oaks of 21-acre Old Maids Woods Preserve leave a lasting impression. Here black oak (up to 42 inches in diameter), white oak, and northern red oak reach 250 years. Their straight vertical trunks average 110 feet in height, with 30- to 40-inch diameters. Hemlocks (with 32-inch diameters) reach 250 to 300 years old. Towering white pine, yellow birch (28-inch diameters), red maple, and sugar maple also grow here. Pitch pines, usually short-lived, modestly sized trees, reach the great age of 220 years and grow to 110 feet in height and 17.4 inches in diameter. The champion black locusts—including one that at 126.6 feet is the Northeast's tallest—grow at the bottom of the hill just outside the ancient part of the forest.

The Nature Conservancy manages the forest, which is owned by the City of Schenectady and named for the two unmarried daughters of an early settler. The daughters inherited the farm, loved the woods, and chose not to log it.

■ **DIRECTIONS**

Take I-890 to Exit 2 at Campbell Road-Rice Road. Follow Rice Road west past the sewage treatment facility to Schermerhorn Road. Turn left and cross under I-890. In 150 feet, turn right on Power Company Road. Park next to the gate.

■ **HIGHLIGHTS**

No permission is needed if you are just visiting the preserve. Walk behind the gate. In 100 feet, turn left onto the forest trail. Pass a sign-in box. Before climbing the hill, look for the towering, champion-height black locusts to the right. When the trail climbs the hill, you immediately enter this ancient forest.

At the top of the plateau, turn left to admire the craggy black and white oaks, soaring pines, and venerable hemlocks. Wander a bit off-trail to find the ancient pitch pines. The trail circles the plateau and loops back to the trail (on your left) that descends the hill to the road.

■ **CONTACT INFORMATION**

Old Maids Woods Preserve, 19 North Moger Avenue, Mt. Kisco, New York, 518-382-5152

67. LITTLE NOSE AND BIG NOSE

The New York Thruway offers one of the Northeast's only examples of a drive-by ancient forest. The expressway and the Mohawk River pass between two steep bluffs, totaling a mile in length, where ancient northern white cedars cling to the 150-foot limestone cliffs of Little Nose and Big Nose.

These twisted white cedars may be more than 500 years old, and they exhibit the bizarre growth forms typical of cliff-dwelling trees: bent trunks that grow downward, then upward, and tangles of roots radiating through the air and into the bedrock.

- **DIRECTIONS**

When driving east on the Thruway (Route 90), watch for Little Nose's cliffs on the right starting at the 190-mile marker. Driving west on the Thruway, starting at the 188-mile marker, look on the right at Big Nose's cliffs, and on the left at Little Nose.

- **HIGHLIGHTS**

To see the forest at close range, take the Thruway to Exit 29 at Canajoharie (5 miles west of the site). Take Route 5S east for 3 miles to the hamlet of Sprakers. Don't take Route 162. Continue on Route 5S for 2 more miles and carefully park off the road. The cliffs are privately owned but you can easily examine them. Use binoculars to see the strange growth forms.

68. SCHOHARIE ESCARPMENT AND VROMAN'S NOSE

The Schoharie Escarpment and neighboring Vroman's Nose offer sights of ragged 200-foot sandstone cliffs harboring bonsai-like red cedars. The oldest probably attain ages of 500 to 900 years. Gnarly dwarf chestnut oak and pitch pine grow on their flat summits.

Near Schenectady, head west on Route 88 to Exit 23. Follow Route 30 south 5 miles to Middleburgh. As you approach the village, you see the towering Schoharie Escarpment on the left. Where Route 30 meets Route 145 in the village, turn left on any side street that heads toward the cliffs.

To visit Vroman's Nose, drive on Route 30 1 mile south of the village. Park here and walk to the bottom of the cliff.

■ HIGHLIGHTS

To see the cedars at the Schoharie Escarpment, bushwhack up the steep slope to the cliff bottom.

The famous Long Path, which runs from Manhattan to the Mohawk River, takes you to the summit of Vroman's Nose. The path begins a bit west on Route 30, on the right. The red trail, after 0.2 mile, climbs to the green trail. Turn right to reach the summit and its spectacular view.

■ CONTACT INFORMATION

New York Old Growth Forest Association, c/o Landis Arboretum, P.O Box 186, Lape Road, Esperance, New York 12066, 518-875-6935

69. WELWYN PRESERVE

One of the Northeast's densest concentrations of ancient tulip trees is only 7 miles from New York City. Forty acres of statuesque tulip trees create their own skyscrapers in Welwyn Preserve. Many surpass 130 feet, and one 144-foot pillar is the tallest accurately measured hardwood tree in southeastern New York. Although most are 24 to 36 inches thick, at least one tulip tree per acre reaches 48 inches in diameter. One 400-year-old forest lord has an astounding diameter of 66 inches, and another four-trunked veteran is 7 feet thick.

The preserve's tulip trees and white oaks exhibit wizened, balding bark and moss carpets. White oaks grow up to 60 inches thick and to 400 years in age. Other ancient species are beech, black birch, and black and northern red oak. Extremely rare river birch also grow here. Welwyn's exquisite woods are a mix of original and secondary old growth, which began developing after nineteenth-century selective logging.

Welwyn is the former estate of Harold Irving Pratt, son of Charles Pratt, a nineteenth-century oil baron and philanthropist. His 1912 Georgian-style mansion is now the Holocaust Museum of Nassau County, on the edge of the preserve. The woods are an example of urban old growth, with exotic plants such as English ivy, periwinkle, and euonymus that escaped from the mansion grounds.

■ **DIRECTIONS**

Take Long Island Expressway (Route 495) to Exit 39. Head 6.2 miles north on Glen Cove Road. Bear left at a major fork and turn right on Brewster Street Glen Cove. Go 0.5 mile and turn left on Dosoris Lane. Drive 0.7 mile to New Woods Road. Turn right on Crescent Beach Road and right again at the entrance gate.

■ **HIGHLIGHTS**

Walk through the gated entrance and turn left onto Trail #1. Head north past the tulip trees and rhododendrons. Paralleling a stream on your right, you pass the ruins of a home. At the fourth footbridge, turn right. You leave the tall forest and in 0.2 mile, reach the old shore drive, now Trail #3. Turn right and detour onto the sand beach and jetty. Trail #3 soon curves rightward along a salt marsh, rich with birds such as osprey, great blue herons, and snowy egrets.

Just before a gate, turn right (away from the bay) where Trail #3 enters the woods. Pass Turtle Pond, then look for the rare river birch with shiny, red-brown curling bark. Where Trail #3 meets Trail #2, turn left. Reenter the ancient forest. In a half mile, Trail #2 ends at Trail #1. Turn left, walking under the tallest tulip trees, almost 150 feet tall. Trail #1 winds around and returns to the entrance on your left.

■ **CONTACT INFORMATION**

Nassau County Department of Parks and Recreation, Eisenhower Park, East Meadow, New York 11552, 516-571-8500

70. Shu Swamp

Within the Shu Swamp region of the 64-acre Charles T. Church Nature Sanctuary, 25 acres of giant tulip trees, up to 54 inches in diameter and 300 years in age, shoot up 120 to 140 feet. Their deeply fissured and balding bark is clothed in banks of moss and cables of large vines.

Black gum (tupelo) growing here are only 2.5 feet in diameter, but are 250 to 450 years old and have distinctive "alligator skin" bark. Old-growth American beech, white oak, white ash, and rare sweetbay magnolia also grow in Shu Swamp. A preserve since 1929, this area is owned by North Shore Wildlife Sanctuary.

Take Long Island Expressway (Route 495) to Exit 39N. Head north on Glen Cove Road to Northern Boulevard (Route 25A). Turn right on Route 25A. Drive 3.2 miles, turn left, and follow Wolver Hollow Road to Chicken Valley Road. Turn right, drive 1.6 miles and turn right on Frost Mill Road (Mill Neck Road). Go 0.3 mile to a T-intersection, and turn left again. Drive 0.5 mile to the preserve entrance on your left.

■ **HIGHLIGHTS**

Take the trail from the north end of the parking lot. Cross a footbridge overlooking a pond with giant carp and follow the trail into ancient forest. Parallel a wire fence at the bottom of a hill, then veer left through swamp forest. After that, take trails heading south (upstream), with the stream on your left. Cross the last footbridge on your left at the south end of the preserve, then wind northward to your car.

The sanctuary is closed on Fridays.

■ **CONTACT INFORMATION**

North Shore Wildlife Sanctuary, P.O. Box 214, Mill Neck, New York 11765, 516-671-0283

71. PELHAM BAY PARK

Like Corinthian columns of brown and gray, ancient tulip trees and oaks soar in the 10-acre old-growth forest of the Bronx's Pelham Bay Park. The red, black, and white oaks; tulip trees; and ten other species reach up to 250 years of age in this 2,764-acre city park. Tremendous red oaks have single-trunk diameters of 48.8 to 55 inches. The tulip trees reach diameters of up to 55.7 inches and heights to 130 feet, with balding bark climbing 40 feet up. White oaks grow to 34.1 to 44.9 inches thick, and black oaks with balding bark are 36 to 44 inches thick.

The rarest tree is old-growth post oak, growing on the rocky shore. Other ancients are black birch, swamp white oak, chestnut oak, red maple, white ash, sycamore, black cherry, and possibly sassafras and bitternut hickory. Even huge old-growth sugar maple, horse chestnut, and sweet cherry grow around a former homestead.

Once the colonial estate of Thomas Pell, the park also features rare native wildflowers. Great horned owl and red-tailed hawks nest here, and visitors even spot long-ear and saw-whet owls.

■ DIRECTIONS

In the Bronx, take Hutchinson River Parkway to the exit for Orchard Beach-City Island. Follow all signs for Orchard Beach, and park at the far left end (northeast) of the huge lot.

■ HIGHLIGHTS

Walk toward the shore, passing tennis courts on your right. At a four-way junction of wide walkways, go straight onto the gravel path, toward the shore. The trail then veers left, paralleling the shore on your right. Pass a sign for Hunters Island Sanctuary.

Along the beginning section of the woods trail you'll see scattered large trees, 130 to 200 years old. Count how many trails you pass on the left. Turn left on the fourth left-hand trail, which is 20 feet after the remnant of an old stone-block colonial wall. Colossal tulip trees immediately surround you. At the next trail, turn right. In 200 feet, pass the largest red oak.

Rejoin the main trail. Turn left and parallel the shore. At the first wide trail, turn left, leaving the forest. After crossing the old stone wall again, you'll reach a fenced-in area of a former residence with old planted trees around it. Later, look for the orange-brown trunks of a sassafras grove on your right.

To return to the parking lot, turn right on a paved trail. To wander the interior trails, turn left. The farther north you go, the older the forest gets. Keep the bay to your left so you'll know which way to return.

■ **CONTACT INFORMATION**

Pelham Bay Park, 1 Bronx River Parkway, Bronx, New York 10462, 718-430-1890

72. MARSHLANDS CONSERVANCY

As its name suggests, the 170-acre Marshlands Conservancy features an expansive, undisturbed salt marsh. It also boasts nine ancient tree species in 15 to 20 acres of exquisite forest. The largest is a 49-inch-diameter black oak with balding bark and a buttressed trunk. A 48-inch white oak is 275 years old. The largest tulip tree is 46 inches in diameter and about 225 years old. Other ancients are American beech (up to 38 inches in diameter), black birch, red oak, red maple, and sweet gum. Even rare ancient post oaks grow on islands in the marsh. A 4-foot-thick chestnut log, 175 years old when it died of chestnut blight around 1910, is still intact. The preserve includes the 23-acre estate of Revolutionary War hero John Jay.

■ **DIRECTIONS**

Take I-287 to Exit 11 at Rye-Route 1. Go south on Route 1. The preserve entrance is the first left after the Rye Golf Club.

■ **HIGHLIGHTS**

Pick up a trail map at the visitor center. The trail to the ancient forest begins to the right of the building. After passing through the big trees, the trail loops and returns along a field. Note the large old planted specimens from the old estate, including a rare English oak.

■ **CONTACT INFORMATION**

Westchester County Parks, Recreation and Conservation Department, 25 Moore Avenue, Mt. Kisco, New York 10549, 914-864-7000

73. ALLEY POND PARK AND THE QUEENS GIANT

New York City's largest living "creature," a 400-year-old tulip tree known as the Queens Giant, is located only 200 feet from the Long Island Expressway in the northwest corner of 635-acre Alley Pond Park. The tree is 69 inches in diameter and 133.8 feet tall, giving it a volume of 1,750 cubic feet—equivalent to 46,000 pounds. It oversees a several-acre ancient grove with other giant tulip trees, northern red oaks, white oaks, and beech trees.

One section of the park, south of the Long Island Expressway, harbors mature second-growth forest mixed with original old-growth beech and red and white oak trees in a beautiful setting of glacial moraine hills and ponds.

■ **DIRECTIONS**

From the Long Island Expressway in Queens, take Exit 31. Follow Douglaston Parkway south. After passing a shopping mall, Douglaston Parkway curves down a hill. Take the right fork (Alley Road), and cross over the Cross Island Parkway. Stay in the right lane, make a right, and pass over the Long Island Expressway. Bear right onto East Hampton Boulevard and immediately stop. Park along the fenced-in woods on your right.

■ **HIGHLIGHTS**

Walk down East Hampton Boulevard, keeping the fence and woods on your left. Just before you cross the bridge over Long Island Expressway, turn left on a paved trail that curves down between the fence and the highway. The "Trail Closed" sign applies to bicyclists only. In only 40 feet, the fence ends. Turn left on a path into the woods. You are now in the urban old-growth grove. In 400 feet, you reach the Queens Giant, surrounded by a broken-down fence. Continue on the trail to admire other remarkable gnarly and knobby ancient trees before entering younger forest.

■ **CONTACT INFORMATION**

New York City Parks and Recreation, The Overlook, Forest Park, Kew Gardens, New York 11415, 718-520-5900

74. GARTH WOODS

Garth Woods, a half-mile, 15-acre corridor of huge trees, parallels the Bronx River Parkway. It's easy to drive by these woods, but we hope you will see it by walking. Tulip trees 4.5 feet thick and oaks more than 250 years old grow here because local citizens saved the park from destruction when the Bronx River Parkway was built in 1926. Since 1991, the Garth Woods Conservancy has worked to protect this treasure.

■ **DIRECTIONS**

Take Metro North Train Harlem Line to Scarsdale. By car, take Bronx River Parkway north from the city. When you pass Exit 10, you are driving through Garth Woods. Get off at Exit 11 and turn right on Popham Road. Take an immediate left to park in the Scarsdale train station or park on Garth Road, a right turn off Popham Road next to the station.

■ **HIGHLIGHTS**

Cross over the tracks and walk south across Popham Road onto Garth Road. Garth Woods is to the west, behind the apartment building on Garth Road. Head south on the paved trail behind the apartment building. Take side trails to explore, then return to the main trail, which reaches Harney Road. Turn right across the overpass of the parkway's northbound lane. Turn right into an open field. Walk north through the field to a trail that heads back into Garth Woods.

■ **CONTACT INFORMATION**

Garth Woods Conservancy, 97 Montgomery Street, Scarsdale, New York 10583, 914-725-4600

75. Inwood Hill Park

It seems impossible, but ancient forest does survive in Manhattan. Inwood Hill Park boasts 25 acres of old-growth tulip tree and oak forest. It is part of the only natural woodland in Manhattan. Tulip trees more than 200 years old grow up to 4 feet in diameter and exceed 120 feet in height. A metal plaque documents a tulip tree that died in 1936, reportedly 168 feet tall, 6.5 feet in diameter, and 280 years old. It germinated in 1656 when this site was still virgin.

The diversity of trees is notable, especially for a place like Manhattan. Eleven species reach old-growth status here, including a 6-foot-thick cottonwood; northern red, black, white, and swamp white oaks (36 to 42 inches in diameter, 150 to 225 years old); cucumber magnolia (31 inches in diameter); and American beech (38 inches thick). Other veterans are white ash, sugar maple, and chestnut oak. The oldest trees here germinated in the 1700s. This is probably very early secondary old-growth forest. Hemlocks were recently killed by hemlock adelgid insect.

This remarkable forest surrounds the Indian Cave, a rock shelter used for millennia by the Reckawawank tribe. The hill ridge above the forest is Manhattan's highest natural point, 232 feet above the Hudson River. About 2 miles of paved paths wind through the park, which John D. Rockefeller purchased and donated to the city in the 1920s. Prior to that, it was part of the nineteenth-century estate of the Lords (of Lord & Taylor department store fame). Where the old estate once stood, a 4-foot-diameter European beech, gingko, and black locust still grow.

■ **DIRECTIONS**

By subway, take the A train to 207th Street station. Walk west (toward the Hudson River) two blocks. Turn right on Seaman Avenue, go four blocks to its end, and turn left on 218th Street. Enter the park here.

By car, take George Washington Bridge into Manhattan. Immediately exit onto local streets. Head east to Broadway and turn left (north). Drive to West 218th Street. Turn left and find on-street parking.

■ **HIGHLIGHTS**

Walk to the end of 218th Street into the park. Visit the Urban Ecology Center to inquire about a guided tour of the forest. Walk around the pond to the wooded hill on the other side. Notice Shorakapok Rock and its plaque. Straight ahead is the ancient forest. Check out the Indian Cave, ahead to your left. Return to the paved walkway at the bottom, and turn left (north). Immediately look for a steep, narrow, and rocky path that cuts diagonally up the hillside under ancient trees.

At the top, the path joins a paved woods trail and leaves the old growth. Turn left, then turn right on a trail to the Overlook Meadow and a vista over the Hudson. Return to the paved trail and turn right. Keep curving left, downhill, back into ancient forest. When you arrive at the meadow and pond, turn right and return to your car.

■ **CONTACT INFORMATION**

New York City Parks and Recreation, Arsenal West, 16 West 61st Street, New York, New York 10023, 212-408-0100

76. New York Botanical Garden Forest

Before the 1980s, the Bronx's 250-acre New York Botanical Garden possessed one of the Northeast's few acknowledged presettlement forests, a 40-acre grove dominated by large black, northern red, and white oaks, as well as tulip trees and hickories, 180 to 300 years old and 24 to 48 inches thick. Some may exceed 120 feet in height. It was once called the Hemlock Grove, but the woolly adelgid insect, introduced to New York in 1985, killed every ancient hemlock. Their stumps show 350 years of annual rings.

The property was purchased by the Lorillards (of tobacco fame) in 1792. In 1884, the city bought it and created the Botanical Garden in 1895.

■ **DIRECTIONS**

Take the Metro North's Harlem Line to the Botanical Garden Station, or take the C or D subway to Bedford Park Boulevard. Walk eight blocks east to the gardens.

■ **HIGHLIGHTS**

Get a map at the entrance. Take Garden Way to Azalea Way. Pass Children's Adventure Garden, then look for the entrance trail into the ancient forest.

From the Orange Trail, take the first left onto the Blue Trail. At the next trail, turn right. When the Blue Trail leaves the forest, turn right and follow the edge of the forest, with gardens on your left. Ten minutes later, take a right and reenter the forest on the Yellow Trail. At the Orange Trail, turn left. At the Bronx River, take the path on your left before the stone bridge to view the lovely gorge.

Then cross the bridge and turn left to see New York City's only waterfall. Recross the bridge, take a left, and pass through more ancient forest. When you exit the forest, turn right on Azalea Way.

■ **CONTACT INFORMATION**

New York Botanical Garden, 200th Street and Southern Boulevard, Bronx, New York 10458, 718-817-8681

77. MIANUS RIVER GORGE

The Hemlock Cathedral, a 53-acre forest graced by two waterfalls during wet periods, is the centerpiece of the 719-acre Mianus River Gorge Preserve. The preserve is the birthplace of the Nature Conservancy, which purchased it in 1955 and now runs 1,600 preserves—the world's largest preserve system. In 1964, Congress designated the Mianus River Gorge, which is named for a Mahican tribe leader killed nearby in 1664, as the nation's first National Natural Landmark.

Grand hemlocks here exceed 350 years and have diameters up to 4 feet and heights of 128 feet. Large tulip trees reach 130 feet and are 225 years old. White oaks and chestnut oaks are 300 to 400 years old. Ancient American beech, black birch, and yellow birch also thrive here.

■ **DIRECTIONS**

Take I-684 to Exit 4. Go east on Route 72 to Bedford Village. From the triangular village green, drive 0.8 mile. At the traffic light, turn right onto Long Ridge (Stamford) Road. Go 0.5 mile, turn right onto Miller's Mill Road, then left on Mianus River Road. Entrance is 0.6 mile on the left.

The red trail starts to the left of the trail map kiosk. Pick up a map. Turn left onto the green trail, which follows the creek into the ancient forest, past Safford Cascade, then back up to the red trail. As you climb out of the gorge, watch on your left for a side trail to the 1700s Hobby Hill Quarry (the 1-mile mark). After admiring the quarry's glistening mica and rose quartz, return to the red trail and turn left. Walk to the Old Growth Overlook and peer down the 200-foot gorge. Farther on, you will reach Havemeyer Falls where the trail ends at Mianus Reservoir, 2.5 miles from your car. On the way back, note the early-1800s stone wall separating the younger forest from the old forest. Follow the blue trail through young forest.

■ CONTACT INFORMATION

Mianus River Gorge Preserve, 167 Mianus River Road, Bedford, New York 10506, 914-234-3455

78. SUNKEN FOREST

Over the centuries, hurricanes have washed away every part of the 84-mile barrier beaches lining the South Shore of Long Island, except in one spot—the 30-acre fairy-tale dwarf woodland called the Sunken Forest.

One of only two such woodlands in the Northeast, it is an old-growth maritime forest of ancient American holly. Fantastically gnarled, twisted holly and black gum trunks, up to 16 inches thick and 250 years old, form a low canopy sculpted by salt sea air. Contorted sassafras also grow with shadbush, red cedar, black oak, pitch pine, black cherry, and red maple. The trees create a gnarly frame for tangles of prickly catbrier, wild grape, Virginia creeper, and, yes, poison ivy.

The forest is part of the pristine 32-mile-long Fire Island National Seashore. It includes New York State's only federally designated Wilderness Area, an 1858 lighthouse, and the 1712 William Floyd Estate.

■ **DIRECTIONS**

From New York City, take Southern State Parkway to Exit 44E. Proceed 4.5 miles on Sunrise Highway. Turn right on Lakeland Avenue. Drive 2 miles to Sayville. Turn left on Main Street. Follow Fire Island Ferry signs. In 0.2 mile, take the first right onto Foster Avenue. Drive 0.6 mile to Terry Avenue and turn left. In one block, turn right. Park in the lot on your right. Take the Sailors Haven Ferry. Call 631-589-8980 for schedules and rates, since the ferry has very limited service.

■ **HIGHLIGHTS**

From the Fire Island Visitor Center, get a guide for the 1.5-mile Sunken Forest boardwalk trail. Insect repellant is a must.

■ **CONTACT INFORMATION**

Fire Island National Seashore, 120 Laurel Street, Patchogue, New York 11772, 631-289-4810

79. Wolfe's Pond Park

Staten Island, New York City's least-known borough, harbors five secondary old-growth groves. The best of these is Wolfe's Pond Park's 10-acre ancient forest. Here, 200- to 300-year-old tulip trees (up to 48 inches thick), beech, and northern red, black, and white oaks thrive in a seldom seen ravine.

■ **DIRECTIONS**

From Staten Island Ferry, take the Staten Island Rapid Transit to Prince's Bay Station. Walk south (toward the bay) on Seguine Avenue to Hylan Boulevard. Turn left, walk to the park entrance, and follow the park road to the last lot.

By car, take Staten Island Expressway to West Shore Expressway (Route 440 South) to Bloomingdale Road exit. Turn left on Bloomingdale. Go 2 miles and turn left on Amboy Road. Drive 0.75 mile and turn right on Seguine Avenue. Turn left at Hylan Boulevard. Drive 0.5 mile to the park entrance. Park at the end of the last lot, in the corner away from the bay.

■ **HIGHLIGHTS**

Take the wide path to the pond and turn right into the woods. Turn left at the next path; cross the brook (this can be challenging during high water). Admire the huge knobby 300-year-old tulip trees in the brook valley.

Ascend the slope and take the first left. Pass the massive, 62-inch-thick black oak, twisted and leaning over the ravine. Soon you'll see the pond through the trees. Turn right at the next path. Stay right at the next fork. At the next four-way trail junction, turn right. Head downhill, then turn left at the next path. (If you reach the brook, you passed the trail.)

This path descends to the brook, but don't cross it. Turn right and follow the edge of the brook on a faint path. Soon, 50-foot ravine banks and tulip trees tower over you. At the next trail, turn left, cross the brook and turn right. Look for white egrets and herons, which frequently visit the pond in this 316-acre park.

■ **CONTACT INFORMATION**
Wolfe's Pond Park, 80 Mann Avenue, Staten Island, New York 10314, 718-761-7496

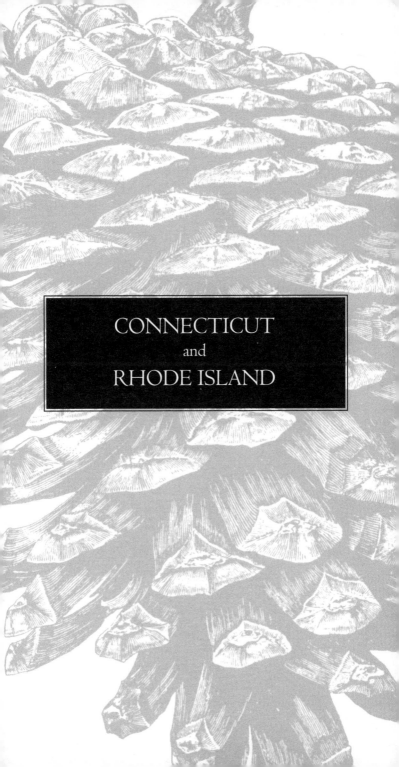

CONNECTICUT
and
RHODE ISLAND

As two of America's smallest states, with a 350-year history of forest cutting, Connecticut and Rhode Island retain very little of their original old-growth trees. All told, these two states have only 100 to 200 acres of ancient forest—less than 0.01 of 1 percent of their total forest acreage. Most of this is in Connecticut's northwest corner, including Cathedral Pines, which was once New England's best ancient forest. Unfortunately, a violent thunderstorm blew down all but 8 acres of it in 1989.

Of ten known old-growth sites, half are original forest and half are secondary old growth. They are equally distributed on state land and nonprofit nature preserves. However, due to a lack of a thorough state inventory, the actual acreage is uncertain. Until 1980, Cathedral Pines was considered Connecticut's only surviving old-growth site.

We suspect there are at least a half dozen other scattered pockets of old-growth forest on private lands and on the basalt ridges of the Connecticut River Valley. We have observed very old hemlock, black birch, and northern red, white, and black oak stands on the dry ledges east of the Farmington River near Simsbury. They are likely to be a mix of secondary and original old growth, but fires have obliterated the distinction between the two categories.

Rhode Island, only the size of New York's St. Lawrence County, has just two known old-growth sites, and both are newly discovered. The only previously known site, Ell Pond, was devastated by the hemlock woolly adelgid insect.

While old-growth forest is rare in Connecticut, the state ranks high in champion and historic individual trees of the Northeast. Connecticut was noted for America's best-known historic tree, the Charter Oak, until it blew down in 1857. In 1662, England's King Charles II granted Connecticut a charter for self-government in a ceremony under this tree, which was 10.5 feet in diameter and probably 500 years old. Connecticut claims 6 national champions—sugar maple, butternut, black oak, bear oak, gray birch, and European larch—and 125 New England champions.

80. CATHEDRAL PINES

For decades, New England's quintessential virgin forest was Connecticut's famous 42-acre parcel known as the Cathedral Pines. It was probably New England's tallest forest, with trees up to 172 feet. Then a 1989 thunderstorm blew down all but 8 acres.

Today, you can still get a sense of the original forest cathedral in a grove of white pines that create a canopy over hemlock, northern red oak, sugar maple, white ash, red maple, and yellow and black birch. Our research verifies this stand as a mix of original and secondary old growth, with presettlement hemlocks more than 300 years old and postrevolutionary pines between 200 and 225 years old. The largest surviving tree is almost 139 feet tall and has a 44-inch diameter.

The pines have been protected since 1883, when John Calhoun bought the tract to prevent it from being lumbered. His family deeded it to the Nature Conservancy in 1968. Because the Conservancy refused to allow "salvage" logging after the 1989 storm, those fallen trees now serve as nurse logs, microhabitats, nutrient supply, and wildlife cover.

■ DIRECTIONS

From I-84 in Waterbury, take Route 8 north to Exit 44. Follow Route 4 west for 13 miles to Cornwall. When you reach Route 125, turn left. In 0.4 mile, turn left again. In 0.2 mile, bear left at the next fork to remain on Essex Hill Road. Pass through an area of downed trees and turn left into a tiny parking area marked with a sign.

■ HIGHLIGHTS

On the right side of the parking area, the famous Appalachian Trail takes you immediately into the forest cathedral grove. Stop and explore off the trail. If you go a quarter mile farther, you exit the old forest and enter a younger one.

■ CONTACT INFORMATION

The Nature Conservancy, Connecticut Chapter, 55 High Street, Middletown, Connecticut 06457, 860-344-0716

81. BALLYHACK PRESERVE

Sky-piercing white pines, 120 to 130 feet tall and 175 to 225 years old, are the showpieces of the Ballyhack Preserve. They include Connecticut's second tallest tree—a 143.5-foot, 31.3-inch-diameter white pine. Close by, another pine reaches 34.4 inches in diameter.

Besides the pines, hemlocks that are 200 years or older grow in the 25-acre old-growth area in the northern part of the Ballyhack, along with mature sugar maple, red maple, black birch, and northern red oak. These trees range between 150 and 200 years of age.

In 1969, the Nature Conservancy of Connecticut acquired this 56-acre property, which includes this grove of secondary old growth, originally called Woolsie Pines. Prior to 1989, Ballyhack existed in the shadows of Cathedral Pines, a scant mile away. Fortunately, the microburst that destroyed most of the Cathedral Pines didn't do as much damage to the Ballyhack trees.

■ **DIRECTIONS**

Follow the directions given for Cathedral Pines. When Route 4 reaches the center of Cornwall and the junction with Route 125, turn right (north). Head west for a half mile and turn left on Dibble Hill Road. The ravine on your left is Ballyhack. You can park here and walk down into Ballyhack. For easier parking, make the first left onto Ballyhack Road and turn left.

■ **HIGHLIGHTS**

Access to the preserve is immediately on the left. Baldwin Brook is at the bottom of the ravine and parallels Route 125 on the east. Walk downstream on one side of the ravine and return upstream on the other side.

■ **CONTACT INFORMATION**

The Nature Conservancy, Connecticut Chapter, 55 High Street, Middletown, Connecticut 06457, 860-344-0716

82. Sages Ravine and Bear Mountain

Nestled in the northwest corner of Connecticut, Sages Ravine features the state's largest area of ancient forest, 100 acres of old growth, and its tallest mountain. This rugged 600-foot-deep ravine and ancient forest starts in Massachusetts and descends through Connecticut. The Appalachian Trail corridor is on National Park Service lands, and other trails are on state park land.

The most impressive timber is in the three-quarter-mile-long lower part of the ravine. Two waterfalls here created barriers to logging operations that otherwise would have robbed the area of its stately hemlocks. Today's ancient forest has changed little from that seen in photographs taken in the 1890s. Rust-hued hemlocks are 250 to 400 years old. Ancient white pine and yellow and black birch also grow here.

At 2,322 feet above sea level, Bear Mountain is the tallest mountain entirely inside the state of Connecticut. (The neighboring slope of Mount Frissell, 2,380 feet in elevation, is the true highest point). At least 5 acres of old-growth forest adorn Bear Mountain's southeast slope. Its ravine harbors three small stands of very stately ancient hemlocks, up to 110 feet tall and 200 to 350 years in age. Aged black birches also grow here.

Despite this mountain's intense human history, it has regained a kind of wildness. It is fitting that bear oak is common on Bear Mountain, and black bear have returned.

■ **DIRECTIONS**

From Massachusetts Turnpike (I-90), take Exit 2-Lee. Follow Route 102 to Stockbridge and turn left onto Route 7. On the south side of Great Barrington, turn right onto Routes 23 and 41 to South Egremont. Just west of town, turn left, and stay on Route 41 until it crosses the Connecticut state line. Drive 1.6 miles to the hikers parking area on the right. This is Mt. Riga State Park's trailhead, which leads to the Appalachian Trail.

■ **HIGHLIGHTS**

This hike totals 8.1 miles, with an ascent of 1,650 feet. Add up to 2 miles if you choose the demanding bushwhack option.

Follow the blue-blazed Undermountain Trail up the hill. In a mile, the trail swings close to Brassell Brook, on the left. Bushwack into the ravine to get a close view of remnant old growth on the steep sides. Return to the main trail.

Soon you will pass Paradise Lane Trail on your right (you will descend this trail on your return route). Take the left fork up the hill. In 0.4 mile, the trail crosses Brassell Brook. (Bushwhack up the brook if you want to see a small but beautiful grove of ancient hemlocks. Then return to the main trail.) In 0.2 mile after Brassell Brook, you'll reach the junction with the Appalachian Trail. Turn right (north) on the white-blazed Appalachian Trail.

During your 0.8-mile, 500-foot climb up Bear Mountain, watch for contorted, bonsai-like pitch pines on exposed rock ledges. The summit is marked by an imposing stone monument. The abundant bear oak (scrub oak) testifies to past fires. Enjoy excellent vistas of the Catskill, Taconic, and Berkshire Mountains.

From the summit, the Appalachian Trail descends very steeply through second growth. In a half mile, pass Paradise Lane Trail on your right; you will take this on your return trip. A yellow blaze tells when you cross the state line. Soon you descend into Sages Ravine, where picturesque old growth becomes common.

In 0.6 mile, the trail crosses the ravine's brook. At this point, you can either stop and return by the Appalachian Trail or you can leave the trail—through a challenging bush-whack down the steep ravine—to see the best old growth. If you choose to bushwhack, do so at your own risk. The rocks are slippery. Most people turn around when they reach the cascades. The most primeval old growth continues downstream, but the route gets even more treacherous in the 600-foot descent to Route 41. From here, it is a 1.6-mile walk south on Route 41 to your car.

On your return walk, where the Appalachian Trail crosses the state line again, turn left on blue-blazed Paradise Lane Trail. This is the shorter, easier route back, which avoids the climb over Bear Mountain.

At 0.3 mile from the junction, on the northeast side of the trail, you pass Bear Mountain's third area of old-growth hemlock. The hemlocks and scattered black birches probably started after a long-ago fire. The trail passes a wetland and runs through second-growth oak forest. At 2.1 miles from the Appalachian Trail, this spur trail rejoins the Undermountain Trail near the little dam on Brassell Brook. Turn left and you reach your car in 1.2 miles.

- **CONTACT INFORMATION**

Appalachian Mountain Club, 5 Joy Street, Boston, Massachusetts 02108, 617-523-0636

83. MATTHIES GROVE

Two-acre Matthies Grove, a narrow belt of secondary old-growth white pines, is intimate and pretty. The largest pines on the Farmington River reach 128.4 feet, almost 36 inches in diameter, and about 200 years in age.

- **DIRECTIONS**

Where Route 8 ends at Winsted, turn right on Route 44. In 3 miles, turn left onto Route 318. In less than a mile, cross the Farmington River and turn left onto East River Road. Pass the People's State Forest headquarters and park in the Matthies Grove lot on the left.

- **HIGHLIGHTS**

Walk through the belt of young pines all the way to the river shore. Head 300 feet downstream, passing a scattering of large pines. Then walk back upstream 1,000 feet until the big pines end. Return the way you came.

- **CONTACT INFORMATION**

People's State Forest, P.O. Box 1, Pleasant Valley, Connecticut 06063, 860-379-2469

84. GOLD PINES

Gold Pines boasts the tallest tree in the state—a 144.6-foot-tall, 32-inch-diameter white pine. However, this is not a natural old-growth forest. It is a managed stand—a forestry demonstration project of Housatonic State Forest. Nonetheless, its towering secondary old-growth and mature trees between 125 and 200 years old make the forest a worthy destination in a state with such a scarcity of old growth.

The largest white pine here is an impressive 43 inches in diameter and 134.1 feet tall. Near the trail is the grove's tallest tulip tree, 127.6 feet tall and 35 inches in diameter. It grows near the northern edge of the species' range.

■ **DIRECTIONS**

Take Route 8 to Torrington. At Exit 44, drive 14 miles west on Route 4. Where Route 4 meets Routes 43 and 128 in Cornwall, go straight on Route 128 for 4 miles. Two miles past the junction with Route 125, turn left into a small parking area with a kiosk with information about Gold Pines.

■ **HIGHLIGHTS**

Walk up the woods road into the tall pines area. Several large black oaks line the road. The champion tulip tree grows on the right side of the main access road midway into the pine grove. Explore the forest on either side of the woods road to see the towering pines. In a quarter mile, you enter mature second-growth forest. Return the same way you came.

CONTACT INFORMATION

Housatonic State Forest, 79 Elm Street, Hartford, Connecticut 06106, 860-424-3630

85. Catlin Woods

Catlin Woods, covering 15 acres of a 30-acre natural area, is a fine choice for an easy walk through secondary old-growth forest.

The woods, part of Litchfield County's prestigious 4,000-acre White Memorial Foundation, has been studied by scientists to understand how old colonial lands transition to forest. The woods was once a mix of colonial pastures and wood lots and has since been growing back and maturing for 200 years.

A few of the hemlocks reach 30 to 38 inches in diameter. The largest trees are old field-grown white pines up to 48 inches in diameter and 116.7 feet tall.

■ DIRECTIONS

From Litchfield, take Route 202 west for about 2 miles to Bissell Road. Turn left and then right into White Memorial Foundation. Drive half a mile to the museum and parking lot.

■ HIGHLIGHTS

Pick up a trail map and find the blue blazes that identify the trail through Catlin Woods. You can also drive down Bissell Road through a small stand of some of the old white pines and hemlocks. The blue-blaze trail crosses the road about a half mile from Route 202.

■ CONTACT INFORMATION

White Memorial Foundation, 80 Whitehall Road, Litchfield, Connecticut 06759, 860-567-0857

86. OAKLAND FOREST

One of Rhode Island's two publicly accessible ancient forest groves is 20-acre Oakland Forest. With some of the largest beech trees in New England, the grove is part of a former estate of the nineteenth-century tycoon Cornelius Vanderbilt.

For years, town arborists were unconvinced that the site was old growth, believing the beeches to be no more than 100 years of age. Now authorities have concluded that the trees, which grow up to 85 feet tall and 40 inches in diameter, are between 200 and 300 years old. White and scarlet oaks and red maple grow up to 3 feet in diameter and 75 feet in height.

■ **DIRECTIONS**

From Providence, take I-195 east 17 miles to Fall River, Massachusetts. Take Exit 8A and go 10 miles south on Route 24 toward Portsmouth. Cross the bridge onto Aquidneck Island into Portsmouth. Where Route 24 separates from Route 138, take Route 138 to the left. Follow it to Union Street in Portsmouth (next to the Rhode Island State Police station). Turn onto Union Street and take the first left onto Carriage Drive. At the end, turn in to a three-car gravel parking area.

■ **HIGHLIGHTS**

Follow the foot trail into the forest.

■ **CONTACT INFORMATION**

Aquidneck Island Land Trust, 790 Aquidneck Avenue, Middletown, Rhode Island 02840, 401-849-2799

MASSACHUSETTS

Shortly after arriving in Massachusetts in the early 1600s, settlers began clearing land for cities, agriculture, and pasture, and they logged the remaining forests for wood products. By the 1850s, nearly 75 percent of the native forest cover in the eastern and central part of the state had been cleared. Historians concluded that all of the Bay State's original forest cover was gone by the early 1900s.

They were wrong. A thorough search revealed that Massachusetts has some notable pockets of high-quality old-growth forest. We have identified fifty-five separate stands of ancient forest totaling approximately 3,700 acres—including areas still being mapped. Only six of the old-growth sites were known prior to the 1980s.

A surprising number of old-growth stands in densely populated Massachusetts are accessible. The public can visit thirty-three sites spread over thirty separate properties. Eighteen properties are public lands (sixteen state and two municipal), and seven properties are nonprofit or college owned. Only five properties are privately owned, and one public property is not open to the public.

87. MOHAWK TRAIL STATE FOREST

Mohawk Trail State Forest is New England's tallest old-growth forest. Nearly 700 acres of old growth cover the steep, 1,300-foot ridges of Mohawk and neighboring Savoy Mountain State Forest, which together total 17,500 acres. The forest's tall tree index averages 133.82 feet in height, almost as high as Pennsylvania's Cook Forest. A total of thirty-one noble white pines exceed 150 feet, with three reaching above 160 feet. Ten ash trees exceed 140 feet.

The other ancient trees here—the hemlock, black birch, white oak, and northern red oak—do not reach such great stature, due to shallow soil, fires, windstorms, and lightning. But they do reach significant ages, ranging from 150 to more than 400 years.

Another feature that distinguishes Mohawk Trail State Forest is that fifteen of its native tree species are state or regional champions of height.

■ **DIRECTIONS**

Take I-91 to Greenfield at Exit 26. Take Route 2 (also called the Mohawk Trail) west for 22 miles to the entrance to Mohawk Trail State Forest, on the right. Pick up a trail map in the park.

Start the Mahican-Mohawk Recreational Trail at the forest headquarters and walk up the paved campground road, which climbs a hill. Passing the park's refuse site on the left, you enter a mature second-growth forest. At the top of the small hill, the road levels, becoming an avenue of beautifully formed tall pine trees. Two trees to your right reach 140 feet and signal the beginning of the tall trees.

Follow the paved road past a leaching field, where you'll see the Pocumtuck pines, named after a native tribe. These pines are the first of four towering groves in Mohawk.

Take the dirt road on the right, leading past the back of a cabin to a group campsite. (You can detour onto Thumper Mountain Trail, which adds a half-mile round-trip to a wide vista over the old growth.) Walk through the campsite past an old CCC fire pond on the left. Just beyond here, you'll find the Trees of Peace, the second grove. The large double-stemmed pine on the right side of the road at the curve is the Calibration Tree (150.1 feet tall, 47 inches in diameter). The tall pines immediately on down the hillside have been named in honor of Chief Arvol Looking Horse, a Lakota currently working for world peace.

Just before the Calibration Tree, a flagged trail leads down past a cluster of four 150-footers on the left, including the 151.7-foot-tall Arvol Looking Horse Tree. Near the sign for the Trees of Peace, an unmarked path on the left leads into the center of the grove. At the lower part of the grove is the 162.1-foot-tall, 38.6-inch-diameter Jake Swamp Pine, Massachusetts's tallest tree, named after the Akwesasne Mohawk chief, the "Keeper of the Trees."

Continue downhill into a meadow and walk east toward the river to the main trail. Turn left and walk north across

Stafford Meadow into a third grove, the Algonquin Pine Grove. Here, ten pines are taller than 150 feet, including the Algonquin Pine (156.6 feet) and the Frank DeContie Pine (152.2 feet), named after a well-known medicine man.

Continue up the steep trail to a 150- to 250-year-old hemlock and black birch forest. Look for striped maples almost a foot in diameter. Near the top of the ridge, northern red oaks are joined by white oaks as old as 250 years. At the saddle in the ridge (elevation 1,460 feet), the Mahican-Mohawk Trail joins the original Mohawk Trail. The left fork goes to a lookout at 1,702 feet and runs mostly through old growth on the northern side. The right fork runs through a 1.1-mile swath of old growth up to the lower knob of Clark Mountain.

When you reach an open field, reverse direction and walk back to the saddle opposite where the trail reached the ridgeline. Turn down the south side to the original Mohawk Trail route. At the bottom, turn left on the paved road and walk back to the park headquarters.

■ **CONTACT INFORMATION**
Mohawk Trail State Forest, Berkshire Office, P.O. Box 7, Charlemont, Massachusetts 01339, 413-339-5504

88. Dunbar Brook–Monroe State Forest

Few Massachusetts forests top the hardwoods on the steep slopes of Dunbar Brook, which features more than 20 acres of ancient and old second-growth woods.

New England's champion forest-grown white ash, 54 inches in diameter and 124 feet tall, grows in Dunbar, along with other giants—a yellow birch 49.5 inches in diameter, a hemlock 48.5 inches in diameter, and a striped maple 9 inches in diameter. Dunbar Brook also has some eye-popping white pines. The Henry David Thoreau White Pine is 47 inches in diameter and 156.2 feet tall. Its uphill neighbor, the Grandfather Tree, is 52.6 inches thick and 142.4 feet tall. Many of these trees are found off-trail.

The most surprising big trees in Dunbar are in the rare stand of old big-tooth aspens near the brook. The Massachusetts champion big-tooth aspen, growing here, is 28.5 inches thick and 112 feet tall. The thick gray corrugated bark of these aged trees is different from the green-white smooth bark of the younger aspens that most people encounter.

■ DIRECTIONS

From the intersection of I-91 and Route 2 (the Mohawk Trail) at Greenfield, drive 17 miles west on Route 2 to the town of Charlemont. From the intersection of Route 2 and Route 8A, drive 2.1 miles west and turn right on River Road. Drive approximately 2.5 miles to the split in the road, and turn left. The road passes under the railroad and then parallels it, eventually crossing the Deerfield River. Continue on River Road across the railroad at Hoosac Tunnel. From there, it's 4 miles to the Dunbar Brook trailhead.

■ HIGHLIGHTS

From the trailhead, stay to the left of the substation, and walk up the hill to a forest of American beech, yellow birch, and sugar maple. Then pass through a dense stand of 125- to 225-year-old hemlock sprinkled with black birch.

In the Dunbar Brook drainage, swaths of old-growth forest send their tentacles down, following the rocky terrain of the boulder fields. This is prime growing habitat, with rocks rich in magnesium, iron, and calcium. You encounter the stand of champion big-tooth aspens farther up the trail.

At 0.6 mile from the trailhead, turn left onto the half-mile-long Raycroft Extension Trail. About 900 feet up the trail, the path cuts sharply to the southeast and up the ridge. New England's forest-grown champion white ash grows just off the trail on the left, inside the trail bend. Follow the trail up to a shelter to see the old-growth stand that extends down this slope.

Return to the main trail, cross the footbridge, and enter a campground. The large 120-year-old pines are scattered up the trail to Haley Brook. Cross the brook and head past another shelter, leaving the old growth. About 1.1 miles from the first footbridge near the Raycroft Trail, you reach Parsonnage Brook. On the uphill (north) side of the trail are ancient red spruce and hemlock with yellow birch, beech, and red maple. The heavy quantity of woody debris that has built up makes the forest floor spongy and therefore fire-resistant. Along the 0.9-mile walk through mature second growth to South Road, you are rewarded with a small waterfall. Beyond it, the trail ends at South Road. Return the way you came.

■ **CONTACT INFORMATION**

Massachusetts Department of Environmental Management, Berkshire Office, P.O. Box 1433, Pittsfield, Massachusetts 01201, 413-442-8928

89. ICE GLEN

With the state's largest collection of hemlocks taller than 120 feet, as well as beautiful ashes and some of the region's largest white pines, the primeval 25-acre Ice Glen is the most accessible, high-quality old growth in New England.

The protection from wind and the cool climate created by the Glen's slopes and abundant moisture allow trees here to grow tall and old. The Glen's hemlocks and white pines have been dated to 300 years of age. One 39-inch-thick, 250-year-old hemlock rises 136.6 feet, making it the tallest hemlock in New England. A 300-year-old white pine at the south end of Ice Glen is New England's second tallest tree, at 153.2 feet in height and 48.5 inches in diameter. Other pines, including the 142.6-foot Monarch Pine, soar above 140 feet. Several ashes here exceed 130 feet.

Red pines, an unusual tree species in Massachusetts, have been dated to more than 200 years of age. They do not grow in the shaded parts of the ravine, but high on the ridges. At the upper edges of the ravine, sugar maple, red maple, and white ash are up to 250 years old.

Ice Glen's trees were spared because the narrow, rocky ravine was too difficult to log. The glen's jumble of rocks, a product of the last period of glaciation, has created a network of cavernous openings that retain pockets of cold air into June. Local inhabitants used to harvest ice here to preserve food, hence the name Ice Glen.

■ **DIRECTIONS**

From Massachusetts Turnpike (I-90), take Exit 2-Lee. Drive on Route 102 to Stockbridge, turn left onto Route 7, and head toward Great Barrington. Go about 0.2 mile and turn left onto Park Street. Drive to its end at the parking lot and trailhead.

■ HIGHLIGHTS

While the trail through the glen is only 0.7 mile, it is not a hike for anyone with weak ankles, because the rocks are slippery when wet. Avoid off-trail scrambling, which damages sensitive flowers and ferns.

Look for New England's champion hemlock in the lowest part of the glen on the downhill side of the trail. On the north side of Ice Glen, notice a towering stand of secondary old-growth pines. Look for the Monarch Pine on the west side of the trail, about 250 feet away.

After touring the Ice Glen, visit the nearby Laura's Hill lookout tower.

■ CONTACT INFORMATION

Laurel Hill Association, P.O. Box 24, Stockbridge, Massachusetts 01262, 413-298-4714

90. Mt. Greylock

Although the rounded summit of Mt. Greylock was cleared for sheep pastures in the 1800s, 450 to 500 acres of ancient forest survive on its steep northern and western slopes.

The 12,500-acre Mt. Greylock State Reservation, part of the Taconic Range along the New York border, harbors old growth in three places—the "Hopper" (which reminded settlers of a grain hopper), the Roaring Brook watershed, and the north side of neighboring Mt. Williams.

The Deerhill and Money Brook Trails pass through the Hopper old-growth forest.

■ **DIRECTIONS**

Take Massachusetts Turnpike (I-90) to Exit 2-Lee and go north on Route 20. North of Lee, Route 7 joins Route 20. Stay on Route 7 through Pittsfield and go 6 miles to the entrance of Mt. Greylock State Reservation. Turn right onto the reservation road and follow it to the park headquarters to pick up a map. From there, follow the road into the reservation for about 6 miles. A left-hand fork takes you to the Sperry Campground, where the trailhead is located.

■ **HIGHLIGHTS**

For the Deerhill Trail, a 1.9-mile loop, start by taking the Roaring Brook Trail past the Circle Trail cutoff on the left. Take the next left onto Deerhill Trail, where the forest of hardwoods becomes noticeably older as you descend steeply into a ravine with sugar maple, northern red oak, hemlock, white ash, and beech. The trail reaches Roaring Brook and its 70-foot waterfall, which freezes in the winter to create a natural ice castle. Large rusty-barked hemlocks are between 225 and 375 years old.

Cross Roaring Brook and climb steeply into a forest of 300- to 350-year-old hemlock and 150- to 250-year-old red spruce. About 2,000 feet after the stream crossing, you reach a small Adirondack shelter. The trail flattens out and passes tall red spruce on the right, including the state co-champion, 30 inches in diameter and 109.4 feet tall. Now enter second-growth hardwood forest. At the trail intersection, take the left fork and walk a half mile to return to Sperry Campground Road.

For the Money Brook Trail, start at Hopper Trail, a road lined with large American basswood, black cherry, and sugar maple. At 0.3 mile, take the left fork onto Money Brook Trail. In 0.4 mile, look on the right for the state champion quaking aspen (33.7 inches in diameter, 85.4 feet tall), impressive for this normally small species.

Shortly after the confluence of Bacon and Money Brooks, leave the main trail to see the New England red spruce height champion. Follow an old logging road up this ravine for a quarter mile, then bushwhack up the stream for another quarter mile to a small waterfall. The red spruce reaches 129.1 feet in height. You will see large hemlocks on the right and a 110-foot, 37-inch-thick basswood at a small split in the stream. A white ash just downhill is even larger (42 inches in diameter, 116.8 feet tall). Old-growth northern red oaks, sugar maples, and hemlocks extend 0.4 mile to the rim of the Hopper. On the ravine's north side is a champion-size striped maple, 14 inches in diameter.

Return down to the Money Brook Trail and take a sharp left onto Mt. Prospect Trail, which climbs to Mt. Prospect's 2,690-foot summit. The heavy, stunted oak covering on the summit resulted from a significant fire in the past. In another 0.4 mile, you'll see a remnant of massive old-growth trees on the left, including a 52.6-inch-thick, 102-foot-tall red oak. In another 0.4 mile, arrive at lovely Money Brook Falls, which is surrounded by 25 acres of virgin forest, including hemlocks up to 250 and 350 years old.

■ CONTACT INFORMATION

Mt. Greylock State Reservation, P.O. Box 138, Lanesborough, Massachusetts 01237, 413-499-4262

91. William Cullen Bryant Estate

. . . enter this wild wood and view the haunts of Nature.
The calm shade shall bring a kindred calm, and
the sweet breeze that makes the green leaves dance,
shall waft a balm to thy sick heart.

Inscription for "The Entrance to a Wood"

American poet William Cullen Bryant (1794–1878) grew up in the central Berkshires, where he developed a deep affection for the country and was inspired to write works such as "Forest Hymn," "Autumn Woods," and "The Rivulet." Many of the ancient hemlock, sugar maple, red maple, white ash, and yellow birch of the Bryant Estate's 25-acre ancient forest date back to the time of his childhood, making these special trees more than 200 years old. There are also more large-girth, tall white pines concentrated in this area than in any other Massachusetts forest.

■ DIRECTIONS

From Interstate 91, take Exit 19-Northampton. Drive 21 miles west on Route 9 to the village of Cummington. Just beyond Cummington, take Route 112 south. Drive 1.5 miles to the Bryant Estate at Four Corners. Take the gravel road directly ahead into the estate. Pick up a trail map.

■ HIGHLIGHTS

The Rivulet Trail starts on the right and passes through a scraggly area of regrowth forest. After a short distance, the trees become much larger and older. The trail makes a left turn and enters an area of impressive trees, including a 33-inch-thick black cherry. At the lower end of the trail, Bryant's poem "The Rivulet" is posted. Where the trail circles to the left and nears a small bridge before turning back uphill, large sugar maples surpass 300 years of age.

At the western end of the trail, you'll see another trail heading into a stand of mature pines up to 155.4 feet in height and 46 inches in diameter. The eastern section has young pines, reaching to 146 feet in height and 44 inches in diameter. The trail winds through the big pines and rejoins the Rivulet Trail. Return the way you came.

- **CONTACT INFORMATION**

Trustees of Reservations, 522 Essex Street, Beverly, Massachusetts 01915, 978-921-1944

92. MT. EVERETT

The dwarf Tolkien forests of Mt. Everett and Mt. Race suggest an oriental landscape of bonsai forms. Within a 13,000-acre state park, the dome-shaped Mt. Everett rises to 2,608 feet, where ice-sculpted pitch pine, bear oak, gray birch, northern red oak, and red maple vie for dominance. Enhancing this scene are far-off views of Rip Van Winkle country across the Taconics to the distant Catskills.

Mt. Everett's summit is covered in a newly discovered old-growth ecosystem that self-reproduces for many forest generations. A fire, perhaps every few hundred years, allows pitch pines to gain dominance and the cycle starts over again. The dwarf pitch pines here are typically 80 to 170 years old, considered by many ecologists to be old growth for this short-lived species. The understory for the pitch pines is blue-berry. Huckleberries form the understory for the bear oak. The two communities vie with one another for dominance.

■ DIRECTIONS

From Massachusetts Turnpike (I-90), take Exit 2-Lee. Follow Route 102 to Stockbridge and turn left onto Route 7 toward Great Barrington. On the south side of Great Barrington, turn right onto Routes 23 and 41 to South Egremont. Just west of town, turn left to stay on Route 41. Take the first right, just past Mill Pond, onto Mt. Washington Road, which eventually becomes East Street. Follow East Street to the entrance of Mt. Everett State Reservation on the left. Park in the lot.

■ HIGHLIGHTS

From the gate, hike up the woods to an Appalachian Trail sign at a clearing. This is where you will take the Guilder Pond Trail later. From here, you ascend 500 feet in 0.7 mile to the summit. Near the top, you are surrounded by the rare mountaintop dwarf forest of pitch pine and oak.

To return, look for the Return to Car sign painted on the summit rocks. Follow this down for a different route. The trail descends, crosses the woods road, and meets the trail clearing with the Appalachian Trail sign. Take this trail. The Guilder Pond Trail forks to the left off the Appalachian Trail in only 600 feet

Drive to the lot near Guilder Pond for the next flat, 0.9-mile hike. A 15-acre swath of old-growth hemlock, black birch, white pine, and northern red oak grows on the western side of the pond. The first 700 feet of the 1-mile trail are through a hemlock-dominated stand with trees 120 to 200 years of age. Then the hemlocks appear larger and craggier and are 250 to 300 years old. The black birch and northern red oak are 150 to 250 years old, and the mountain laurel is up to 125 years old. A few white pines appear to be 150 to 200 years old. A gently sloping rock at the north end of the pond is an excellent place to absorb the rays of the sun while enjoying a great view of Mt. Everett.

■ CONTACT INFORMATION

Massachusetts Department of Environmental Management, Berkshire Office, P.O. Box 1433, Pittsfield, Massachusetts 01201, 413-442-8928

93. WACHUSETT MOUNTAIN

Many of the twisted oaks and birches that were 200 years old when Thoreau walked up Wachusett Mountain in the 1850s still grow on its 2,006-foot summit today.

A 220-acre bandanna of old growth follows the rock ledges that encircle the upper 500 vertical feet of the mountain. On northern exposures, 150- to 350-year-old dwarfed northern red oak and beech grow near the summit. Beneath the summit, yellow birch up to 369 years old, along with hemlock, sugar maple, red maple, and red spruce populate the north slopes, while red oaks, shagbark hickory, American beech, and white ash cover south exposures.

Trees on Wachusett Mountain reach a maximum of 36 inches in diameter, and old-growth features include stag-head tops, created by repeated ice and wind damage, and balding or deeply furrowed or shaggy bark.

This mountain was sacred to the Nipmuck Indians, but early white settlers timbered and pastured the mountain's lower slopes, while later generations slashed its ancient forests for ski trails and an unsightly antenna farm on the summit. Naturalists and resource managers did not recognize the old growth until May 1995.

■ **DIRECTIONS**

Take I-91 north of Greenfield to Route 2 east. Drive to Route 140 at Westminster and head south on Route 140 for 2.3 miles. Turn right on Mile Hill Road (Park Road). Wachusett Lake is on your left. Go 1.8 miles to the park entrance on the right. Pick up a trail map at the park office.

■ **HIGHLIGHTS**

Starting at the visitor center, our suggested route is 2 miles long. Follow the Bicentennial Trail to the Loop Trail. Go right on the Loop Trail to the Jack Frost Trail. Turn left and go downhill through old hemlock forest with 300-year-old red oaks and hemlocks. Turn right onto the Lower Link Trail, where you leave the old growth. Walk to the junction with the Harrington Trail and turn right. Reenter ancient forest, climbing steeply to the summit for exceptional views. At the summit, take the Old Indian Trail down the mountain. Turn right onto the summit road and walk downhill back to the parking lot.

■ **CONTACT INFORMATION**

Wachusett Mountain State Reservation, Mountain Road, Princeton, Massachusetts 01541, 978-464-2987

94. BULLARD WOODS

Bullard Woods is a 5-acre big-tree haven featuring unforget-table white pines. One with fused trunks is 75 inches in diameter. A nearby single-trunk pine is 51 inches in diameter and 130.4 feet tall. Other pines are up to 130 feet tall and 30 to 40 inches in diameter. Tulip trees, rare in the Berkshires, are as large as 43 inches in diameter and 121 feet tall in Bullard Woods, which is a remnant of a much larger ancient forest. Other impressive trees include hemlocks (40 inches in diameter, 112 feet tall), white ash (45 inches in diameter, 116 feet tall), and northern red oak (38 inches in diameter, 106 feet tall). Ages of trees here are more than 200 years, and some are more than 300 years old.

■ **DIRECTIONS**

Take I-90 to Exit 2. Go on Route 20 north through Lee. Just after Route 7 joins Route 20, take Route 183 through Lenox toward Tanglewood Concert Center. About 1.5 miles beyond Tanglewood, turn left onto Hawthorne Road. Drive past a large field with a lake in the distance. Continue to the inter-section with a road on the left. The distance is about a half mile from Route 183. At the intersection, Bullard Woods is on the right across a meadow. Park along the main road.

■ **HIGHLIGHTS**

A trail leading south across the meadow becomes an old log-ging road turned into a trail. A large sign at the edge of the pines marks the beginning of Bullard Woods. The trail winds a half mile through the woods. (If you come during the sum-mer, when the Tanglewood Festival is playing nearby, you can hear music wafting through the woods.) While many of the big trees are visible from the trail, you must wander off the main trail to see the big pines. Return the way you came.

■ **CONTACT INFORMATION**

Stockbridge Bowl Association, P.O. Box 118, Stockbridge, Massachusetts 01238, 413-298-4714

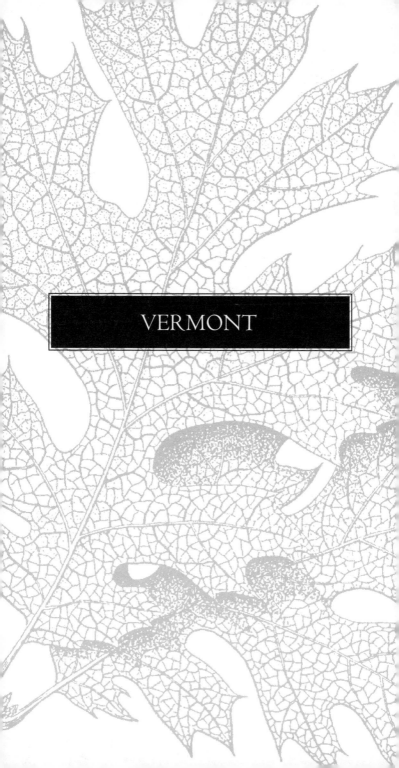

VERMONT

Vermont is known for trees—the deep green forests of the mountains, the brilliant woods with their famous autumn foliage, and maples that are tapped for the syrup that is sent around the world. In spite of its lush forests, however, the state is not known for its ancient trees. Intensive forest management, logging, and agriculture eliminated nearly all of the original forest by the mid-1900s. The acreage of all currently known old-growth sites in Vermont totals only half that of neighboring Massachusetts. But Vermont, a state with so many rugged ravines, steep hillsides, and wild areas, must have at least as many old-growth sites as Massachusetts. We believe a thorough search will uncover up to two dozen more stands of ancient forest.

Of Vermont's fifty-five current old-growth sites, twenty-five are lower-elevation big-tree stands that cover a total of 1,100 acres. Fifteen are northern hardwoods and hemlock, sometimes with spruce. Five are white pine or red pine stands. The two white pine stands, Cambridge Pines and Fisher-Scott Pines, have the most impressive trees. Three sites possess ancient cliff-dwelling northern white cedar with gnarled trunks, and one lowland ancient forest is made up of rare, medium-size black gum.

The remaining thirty sites are all dwarfed thickets covering approximately 1,000 acres on Mt. Mansfield (Vermont's highest, at 4,393 feet), Mt. Killington, Camel's Hump, Jay Peak, and Pico Peak. These forests are 3- to 12-foot-tall dense mats of red and black spruce and balsam fir. The summits of Mt. Mansfield, Camel's Hump, and six other peaks also possess 234 acres of virgin (nonforest) alpine tundra.

Of twenty-seven sites with known ownership, mostly lower-elevation sites, fourteen are state owned, four are part of Green Mountain National Forest, five are nonprofit or college preserves, three are private and unprotected, and one is town owned.

95. CAMBRIDGE PINES

The massive white pines of this 22-acre grove, one of Vermont's finest, create a peaceful stillness in this preserve and neighboring cemetery. The pines here reach 54 inches in diameter, and the largest hemlock, 51 inches in diameter, is probably older than 300 years. Other ancient species include sugar maple (36 inches in diameter), yellow birch, and American beech.

While the large hemlocks are old growth, the age of the white pines is debated. Some maintain that they are second growth, having grown up on a meadow in the 1800s. The town was first settled in the early 1770s.

Cambridge Pines was acquired by the cemetery owners in 1913, purchased by the state in 1944, and declared a State Natural Area in 1965, as part of Cambridge State Forest. Almost no timber has been removed since 1860.

■ **DIRECTIONS**

Take Interstate 89 north of Burlington to Exit 15. Take Route 15 (East Allen Street) east for 24 miles to Cambridge. Go exactly 0.3 mile past the village center. Just after you cross the bridge over the Lamoille River, turn left onto Bartlett Hill Road. Drive 0.1 mile and make a right turn (road still labeled Bartlett Hill Road). Go 0.2 mile up a steep hill to the first red farmhouse and red-roofed barn (mailbox "253") on your left. In front of the home, turn left onto a gravel road. The road angles sharply into the hidden Mountain Cemetery. Drive through the cemetery gate, and bear right on the dirt road, following the right margin of the cemetery. When the road ends, continue driving on the grass to the right corner at the far end of the cemetery. Park here.

■ **HIGHLIGHTS**

To the right of your car, where the fence ends, enter the woods on a faint path. You encounter the largest trees on a steep bank. Carefully climb down and cross the brook to wander through the bottom of this sheltered cove, circling the valley around to your left. Keep the brook and the cemetery slope to your left. Halfway around the slope's other side, climb back up the hill. Explore to find the oldest gravestones.

■ **CONTACT INFORMATION**

Vermont Department of Forests, Barre District Office, 324 North Main Street, Barre, Vermont 05641, 802-476-0174

96. MT. MANSFIELD AND BINGHAM FALLS

Vermont's 4,393-foot-high Mt. Mansfield boasts the state's most extensive alpine tundra, as well as a subalpine zone of virgin dwarfed red spruce and balsam fir, only 2 to 8 feet tall. The 230-acre alpine tundra, another kind of virgin plant community, harbors delicate, rare wildflowers whose usual habitat range is in the Arctic. Its tallest "tree" is a willow that grows only 5 inches tall. The distinct, foot-wide, round patches or rings of rock lichen in this area may be up to 1,000 years old.

The mountain's only known big-tree ancient forest can be seen at Bingham Falls, an exquisite series of cascades through a very narrow gorge. Along the trail and cliffs, admire the ancient hemlocks, 18 to 36 inches in diameter and up to 400 years old. Daniel's Notch State Natural Area protects an old-growth forest (no trail) on the north side of neighboring Sterling Mountain.

- **DIRECTIONS**

Take Interstate 89 to Exit 10-Waterbury-Stowe (the Ben & Jerry Ice Cream stop) and follow Route 100 north. In 10 miles, you reach Stowe; turn left onto Route 108 north. In 5.6 miles, a left turn into the Stowe Ski Resort will take you up Mt. Mansfield Toll Road. But before you do this, see Bingham Falls, another 0.75 mile ahead on the right. To return to the toll road, head south again. Mt. Mansfield Toll Road is a steep, 2,000-foot ascent. When you reach the summit parking lot, turn right and park at the end, where the trail begins.

■ **HIGHLIGHTS**

From the Bingham Falls parking lot, follow the trail down to the gorge. Admire the series of cascades, but don't miss the ancient hemlocks along the edges and walls.

From the Mt. Mansfield parking lot, walk north on the white-blazed Long Trail. Pass through dwarf subalpine spruce and fir and patches of alpine wildflowers. The vistas are the best in Vermont, with views of Mt. Washington, 80 miles to the east, and the Adirondacks to the west. Along the 2-mile route to the summit, watch on the left for a sign to the Subway, and on the right for Cave of the Winds. These crevice caves make excellent short-but-strenuous side trips. The Chin, the highest peak and the largest area of alpine tundra, is exactly 1 mile farther. Return the way you came.

■ **CONTACT INFORMATION**

Vermont Department of Forests, Parks, and Recreation, 103 South Main Street, Waterbury, Vermont 05671, 802-241-3682

97. WILLIAMS WOODS

Williams Woods is the best of the two surviving original forests of the Champlain Valley. The 25-acre old-growth section is amazingly diverse, with fifteen species of ancient trees. Hemlock is the most common and the oldest, up to 300 years. Bur oaks are up to 275 years old. One yellow birch is 182 years old, and a white ash is 140. Sugar maple, beech, red maple, white pine, and white oak are also common. Unusual species are black birch, red spruce, and American elm. Although ancient, most are modest in size, from 18 to 36 inch-es in diameter. The largest is a 45-inch-diameter white ash.

The forest has been undisturbed for the last 100 to 120 years. The previous owners used it only as a firewood sup-ply, and the Nature Conservancy acquired the 63-acre na-ture preserve in 1983.

■ **DIRECTIONS**

From the junction of Routes 22A and 7 just north of Ver-gennes, drive north on Route 7 for 5 miles. Turn left on Stage Road in North Ferrisburg (Ferrisburg Post Office is on the southwest corner), and drive 1 mile to Greenbush Road. Turn right and drive 1.2 miles. As you get close to the woods, you pass a long field on your left. The woods are at the end of this field, beyond the obscure preserve sign. Park on the side of the road.

■ **HIGHLIGHTS**

Follow the easy 1-mile loop trail.

■ **CONTACT INFORMATION**

The Nature Conservancy, 27 State Street, Montpelier, Ver-mont 05602, 802-229-4425

98. WILLMARTH WOODS

Willmarth Woods is one of the state's largest and best stands of old-growth beech-maple woods. Though the 50 acres of majestic trees are not dense because of grazing and selective cutting in the 1800s, the forest is still an imposing sight. The 36-inch-diameter sugar maples are most striking because of their tall, straight, and branchless trunks. Red oaks grow to 48 inches in diameter. Other ancient trees, ranging between 130 and 220 years of age, include white oak, bitternut hickory, red maple, and shagbark hickory. The woods are part of an 80-acre preserve purchased by the Nature Conservancy in 1991.

■ DIRECTIONS

From Burlington, drive south on Route 7 for 20 miles. Make a right on Route 22A into Vergennes. Drive 9 miles south of Vergennes. Turn left (east) on Willmarth Road. In 0.6 mile, turn left on Mountain Road and park in the first lot on your left.

■ HIGHLIGHTS

From the parking lot, turn right and walk 600 feet along the road to the trail entrance on your left. You will head due east, climbing gradually over the next 0.75 mile. Unfortunately, the wide trail skirts the edge of the big-tree area on your right.

To see the big trees, follow the straight trail for 0.7 mile to where it turns sharply to the left at the base of the mountain. Stop here. (Later, you can take this trail up Snake Mountain.) Now turn right to leave the trail, and head south into the woods. Walk only 500 feet or so, and then turn right again, heading west and gradually downhill through the woods. Try to parallel the trail, keeping it to your right but out of sight. As you descend, you pass impressive maples and oaks. In a half mile, you reach younger forest. Turn right and meet the trail again. Turn right to climb Snake Mountain, a popular hiking and hawk-watching destination, or turn left to return to your car.

■ **CONTACT INFORMATION**

The Nature Conservancy, 27 State Street, Montpelier, Vermont 05602, 802-229-4425

99. Button Point

Windswept and wave washed, Button Point represents a previously undocumented type of ancient forest in Vermont: old-growth northern white cedars on the limestone shore cliffs of Lake Champlain. The lake's 150 other similar cliffs may also harbor ancient cedar communities.

These 300- to 500-year-old white cedars grow twisted or project directly out above the water. Some have upside-down trunks, and the largest reach 3 feet in diameter. The inland portion of Button Point has "conventional" old-growth forest, with hemlocks up to 450 years old, 40-inch white pines at 280 years of age, white oaks to 38 inches in diameter, red oaks to 32 inches, and red pines to 18 inches.

Button Point also features vistas of the Adirondacks, large bedrock fossils, long glacial scratches in bedrock, and outstanding bird life.

Named by British soldiers for its disc-shaped "fossil buttons" (concretions), Button Point was once the nineteenth-century estate of Samuel Avery. The state purchased it in the 1970s as the 253-acre Button Bay State Park.

■ **DIRECTIONS**

Take Route 7 south 20 miles from Burlington and turn right onto Route 22A. Pass through the center of Vergennes. After the bridge over Otter Creek, turn right on Panton Road. One mile after the sign for Button Bay State Park, turn right on

Basin Harbor Road. In 4 miles, turn right on Button Bay Road, passing Lake Champlain Maritime Museum. Shortly after, turn right into the park entrance. Pick up a trail map. Drive to the end and park at the picnic shelters.

■ **HIGHLIGHTS**

Walk 0.3 mile on the road along the lakeshore to enter Button Point peninsula. Stay to your left along the lake bluff. Take a side trail down to the rocky shore to get a close look at overhanging cedars. The peninsula trail passes the nature center. At the end of the wave-swept point, enjoy fantastic panoramas.

To return, make sure to take trails that hug the left shore so you won't miss the taller cliffs and their cedars. After a quarter mile, you arrive at a small embayment. Take the trail heading inland to the main trail and your car.

■ **CONTACT INFORMATION**

Vermont Department of Forests, Parks, and Recreation, 103 South Main Street, Waterbury, Vermont 05671, 802-241-3682

100. KINGSLAND BAY STATE PARK

Four miles north of Button Point, Kingsland Bay features a wilder park with more cliff cedars.

■ **DIRECTIONS**

From Button Bay Park, return toward Vergennes. As Route 22A enters Vergennes, immediately after crossing the bridge over Otter Creek, make the first left onto what becomes Sand

Road. Drive 6.5 miles on Sand Road to Kingsland Bay State Park entrance on your left. Drive down the park drive, get a trail map at the entrance booth, and park.

■ **HIGHLIGHTS**

Walk to Hawley House and then to the lake bluff. Keeping the shore on your left, find the shore trail at the end of the meadow. Explore off-trail to see ancient gnarled cedars. A half mile later, near the end of the point, watch for rough stairs that climb down a ledge, taking you along the wildest and most rugged stretch.

On the eastern side of the peninsula, the trail winds south along Hawkins Bay. When it emerges out of the forest and into a meadow, turn right at the next trail. It crosses the meadow and toward your car.

■ **CONTACT INFORMATION**

Kingsland Bay State Park, 77 Kingsland Bay Park Road, Ferrisburg, Vermont 05456, 800-658-1622 (January-May), 802-877-3445 (summer)

101. Gifford Woods State Park

Sugar maple, Vermont's state tree, is indeed abundant in this state. But grand original sugar maples 300 to 400 years old are scarce—unless you're in 7-acre Gifford Woods.

These showpiece sugar maples are as large as 48 inches thick, and up to 107 feet tall. Hemlocks here are typically 170 to 300 years old, with one measured at 419 years. One beech was dated at 241 years. Other monarchs are white ash

(103 feet), basswood (to 40 inches thick), and American elm (38 inches thick). Other ancient trees are yellow birch, beech, and hop hornbeam.

Gifford Woods was used as a "sugarbush," a grove for maple sap production, until 1910. The state purchased the 114-acre park in 1931. In 1980, Congress designated it a National Natural Landmark, and the state declared it a Natural Area two years later. Unfortunately, the state also constructed Route 100 through the old growth in the mid-1900s, destroying many ancient trees.

■ **DIRECTIONS**

From Rutland, take Route 4 east 12 miles. Turn left (north) on Route 100 and quickly turn left into the entrance of Gifford Woods State Park. Leave your car at the park office.

■ **HIGHLIGHTS**

At the north end of the parking lot, take the Kent Brook Trail for a short distance through part of the ancient grove. When the large trees disappear, reverse direction and walk back to the parking lot. Then walk a short distance along the camp road, which is lined by beautiful old sugar maples. When you reach the end of the large roadside trees, return to the parking lot. From there, walk back out the access road to Route 100. Cross the road and explore (off-trail) the woods on the opposite side, to your left. This is the 7-acre stand where the largest and tallest maples grow.

■ **CONTACT INFORMATION**

Gifford Woods State Park, 34 Gifford Woods, Killington, Vermont 05751, 802-483-2314

102. Fisher-Scott Memorial Pines

Fisher-Scott Memorial Pines protects Vermont's most famous grove of impressive white pines. They are some of the few trees in the state that show the grandeur of presettlement days.

These secondary old-growth trees are as majestic as original pines. The largest is a healthy 46 inches thick, 130 feet tall, and 250 years or older. The tallest pine measured is an impressive 143.5 feet.

This lofty 13-acre stand was loved and admired by Vermont's famous author Dorothy Canfield Fisher (1879–1958), and her descendants gave it to the state in her memory. In 1973 it was designated a National Natural Landmark.

■ **DIRECTIONS**

Take Route 7 north from Bennington for 14 miles to Exit 3. Cross over to Route 7A and head north through Arlington. In 2 miles, just beyond a small bridge, turn left onto Red Mountain Road. Go 0.2 mile, look for the trailhead on the left, and park.

■ **HIGHLIGHTS**

Follow the short trail directly to the pine grove and explore off-trail. Climb into the ravine and follow it downstream and then upstream, until the old trees end. Then climb up the same bank and head into the woods toward the road. Within 500 feet, enter a cove with large hemlock, red oak, and sugar maple. Bear left to reach the nature trail again. Turn right to get to your car.

■ **CONTACT INFORMATION**

Vermont Department of Forests, Parks, and Recreation, 317 Sanitorium Road, Pittsford, Vermont 05763, 802-483-2314

103. QUECHEE GORGE

Carved by the Ottauquechee River, the 200-foot-high sheer walls of Vermont's famous Quechee Gorge harbor an ancient forest of white pine, hemlock, and even red pine.

■ **DIRECTIONS**

Take I-89 north to Exit 1-Route 4. Go 2.4 miles west on Route 4 to the bridge over Quechee Gorge. Park in the lot on the eastern side of the gorge.

■ **HIGHLIGHTS**

First walk on the bridge to enjoy the dizzying view over the gorge. The old growth presents an evergreen, shaggy appearance on the steepest slopes. Then take the trail on the east side to see the rare old-growth red pines. Lastly, head down the opposite side to go down to the river. The only old growth at river level are a few large oaks, but the white water, ledges, and summertime swimming provide their own entertainment.

■ **CONTACT INFORMATION**

Vermont Department of Forests, Parks, and Recreation, 317 Sanitorium Road, Pittsford, Vermont 05763, 802-483-2314

104. Vernon Black Gum Swamp

Vernon Black Gum Swamp is one of Vermont's oldest forests and one of its only ancient black gum stands. Although only 18 to 36 inches in diameter, these trees are up to 435 years old. (Black gum trees attain the greatest longevity, 679 years, of any broadleaf tree in eastern North America.)

The ancient black gum in this 8-acre stand display the most charismatic antique bark of any eastern tree, with knobby rows of alligator skin bark that alternate with balding bark and craggy ridges with 3-inch-deep fissures. On trees that are less than 150 years old, the bark has only narrow and shallow furrows.

A tree of southerly climates, black gum is at its northern limits here. The swamp is unique because southern and northern species, such as red spruce, grow together here.

These black gums (also called tupelo and sour gum) were spared because they produce poor quality wood products. The town of Vernon purchased the swamp in 1973, making it a natural area and part of the town's J. Maynard Miller Municipal Forest. Unfortunately, all the woods around it are aggressively managed and logged, creating a stark contrast with the pristine swamp.

■ **DIRECTIONS**

Take I-91 to Exit 1-Brattleboro. Follow Route 5 north through Brattleboro. Turn right (south) on Route 142, and drive 5.4 miles, through the center of Vernon. Go 1.25 miles farther south, turn right onto Pond Road, and pass under a railroad bridge. About 1.2 miles ahead, turn right onto

Huckle Hill Road. In 1.3 miles, turn right on Basin Road and park at the end.

■ **HIGHLIGHTS**

Take a trail map at the preserve sign and follow the dirt road to your left. Bear right on the trail. At the top of the rise, turn right onto the red High Swamp Trail, which circles the black gum swamp. Ignore two trails on your left, but take the third trail, the Overlook Trail, left. Follow this 0.2 mile uphill to an overlook with views of Mt. Monadnock. From the overlook, turn left onto the Mountain Laurel Trail, which circles the preserve through second-growth white birch and mountain laurel woods. From here, bear right at all trail junctions and you return to your car in about a mile.

■ **CONTACT INFORMATION**

J. Maynard Miller Municipal Forest, 567 Governor Hunt Road, Vernon, Vermont 05354, 802-257-0292

105. SPECTACLE POND RED PINES

Sheltered by beautiful red pines, Indian Point along Spectacle Pond was a scenic site in the mid-1850s. This 20-acre pond and peninsula is now a State Natural Area within Brighton State Park.

Judging by their age, between 110 and 200 years, the red pines are most likely a mix of original and mature second growth. Fires associated with the logging era a century ago probably burned this peninsula, stimulating growth of the younger pines. The largest red pines are 23 inches in diameter and glow with beautiful orange-plated bark.

Take I-91 to northeastern Vermont and Exit 23. Take Route 5 into Lyndonville and turn right on Route 114. In 21 miles, Route 105 joins your road from the left. Stay on Route 114 into the village of Island Pond and turn right onto Route 105 east. In 1.5 miles, turn right at the sign for Brighton State Park. In 0.4 mile, turn left into the park entrance. Ask for a park map and also a "Northeastern Kingdom Nature Trail Map" at the ranger station. Drive into the park and take the fork that goes to campsite 13 and the nature museum.

■ **HIGHLIGHTS**

Check out the nature museum, and then take the 1-mile Shore Trail, which begins between campsites 12 and 13. As the trail veers left along the lake, you enter the red pine forest. The pine peninsula is a perfect picnic point.

■ **CONTACT INFORMATION**

Brighton State Park, 102 State Park Road, Island Pond, Vermont 05846, 800-658-6934

NEW HAMPSHIRE

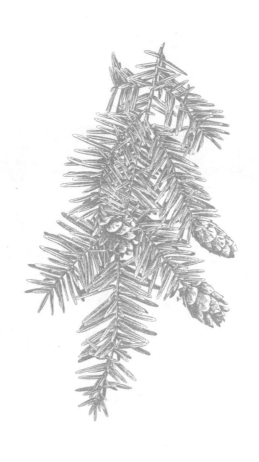

The Granite State of New Hampshire is awash in mountains. Capped by the Northeast's tallest peak, 6,288-foot Mount Washington, the majestic White Mountains dominate the state with sharp ridges punctuated by rocky outcrops.

The mountains possess another notable feature: more than 2,000 acres of big-tree old growth. Another 18,000 acres of dwarf old growth cover the rugged White Mountains, especially on upper mountain slopes and cliffs, subalpine zones, and northern bogs. Yet these thirty-three sites represent only 0.4 of 1 percent of the state's forest.

About 67 percent of the individual sites are on public lands, especially White Mountain National Forest and a variety of state parks and state forests. Almost all the rest are protected in various nonprofit nature preserves. None on our list is owned by private individuals. However, we expect dozens more ancient forests to be discovered on rugged parts of private and public lands in the years ahead.

106. BRADFORD PINES

During the colonial era, among the most prized commodities of the New World were the King's Pines—great white pines cut for use as masts on the ships of Her Majesty's Royal Navy. The Bradford Pines give us a glimpse of what the King's Pines may have looked like.

Although it is only 4 acres, Bradford Pines is New Hampshire's most accessible stand of King's Pines. It features trees whose deeply fissured and plated bark and long, straight trunks are free of limbs for 50 feet or more. The great Bradford Pine is the most impressive tree in this stand, with a volume of about 1,100 cubic feet. The 57.3-inch-diameter monarch soars a dizzying 140.7 feet. Bradford's other pines are almost as impressive; the largest ones average 40 inches in diameter and are almost 130 feet tall.

■ **DIRECTIONS**

From Concord, take I-89 north to Exit 9-Route 103. Drive 8 miles to Bradford. Just after you cross Route 114 (before the center of Bradford), look on the right side for a pull-off, marked by a sign announcing the pines.

■ **HIGHLIGHTS**

A short trail begins 300 feet to the right of the sign. Cross a footbridge and take the left fork. Pass a trail to a burial monument on your right, then enter the grove of pines. To find the largest pine, walk 500 feet on the trail south past the grove and look across the brook to your left. It stands by itself, 150 feet away from the trail.

New Hampshire Division of Parks and Recreation, P.O. Box 1856, Concord, New Hampshire 03302, 603-271-3456

107. MT. WASHINGTON

A landscape of virgin alpine tundra—much like that of the Canadian arctic—is located only 150 miles north of Boston. The 6,610 acres of windswept meadows above timberline on 6,288-foot Mt. Washington include rare arctic plants as well as rock lichen colonies between 500 and 1,000 years old. Thousands of acres of subalpine forest cover steep slopes at 4,000 to 5,000 feet below the alpine zone. Thickets of dwarf red spruce and balsam fir can be more than 100 years old but only 1 to 3 feet tall.

■ DIRECTIONS

Take I-93 to Exit 35. Take Route 3 east, then go on Route 302 east and south. Take Route 16 north to the Mt. Washington Auto Toll Road on the left (summer only). Drive to the summit of Mt. Washington, a steep, 4,000-foot ascent.

■ HIGHLIGHTS

First, see the visitor center and museum, then climb to the rooftop overlook to see the desolate and wild alpine zone. If you plan to hike any distance away from the summit visitor center, bring a map, visit only during the summer, and carry appropriate gear for Mt. Washington's notoriously bad weather, which can include 60-mph winds, sleet, and dense fog in midsummer.

To see the Great Gulf, take the Appalachian Trail. Look for the trail signs on the west side of the summit buildings. Descend and head north across rock and alpine zone. In a quarter mile, pass under the Cog Railway tracks. At the junction with the Gulfside Trail, turn left and walk to the panoramic view over the gulf and its virgin spruce forest. Return or continue toward Mt. Madison.

Also tour the Alpine Garden, the East Coast's most famous alpine zone. Use a trail guide to determine the trail routes; hiking can be rough and strenuous.

■ **CONTACT INFORMATION**

Appalachian Mountain Club, Pinkham Notch Visitor Center, Route 16, P.O. Box 298, Gorham, New Hampshire 03581, 603-466-2721

108. NANCY BROOK NATURAL AREA

Some of the world's oldest red spruce trees—up to 415 years—thrive at the Nancy Brook Natural Area. The trees reach a median age of 254 years, and they grow to 30 inches in diameter and 85 feet in height, very large for this species.

Because of its unique red spruce, 1,385-acre Nancy Brook is an extensively researched old-growth site. Unfortunately, according to a 1986 study, the red spruce here have seriously declined due to acid rain.

■ **DIRECTIONS**

Drive on I-93 north of Concord through dramatic Franconia Notch, where the famous "Old Man of the Mountains" stone profile, the symbol of New Hampshire, broke off in 2003. Route 3 leaves the notch and separates from I-93. Drive 10 more miles and turn right (east) on Route 302. In 8 miles, enter dramatic, 2,500-foot-deep Crawford Notch and stop to admire 250-foot-high Silver Cascade, whose upper slope is primeval forest. After leaving the notch, watch for the Nancy Brook trailhead on the right.

■ HIGHLIGHTS

The 6-mile round-trip Nancy Brook Trail starts off through second-growth forest. As the trail steepens, large old-growth yellow birch and red spruce appear. To explore for the biggest trees, walk off-trail, but stay in Nancy Brook's watershed to avoid getting lost. Large white pines grow on the southern ridge over Nancy Brook.

If you continue on the trail to the summit of Mt. Nancy, you will see old growth that covers all of its slopes and those of its neighboring peaks. The size of the trees decreases as the elevation increases.

■ CONTACT INFORMATION

White Mountain National Forest, 719 Main Street, Laconia, New Hampshire 03246, 603-528-8721

109. PINE PARK

Dartmouth College's 30-acre Pine Park harbors trees up to 152 feet tall, making them the tallest in the state of New Hampshire.

In his 1950s classic *A Natural History of Trees of Eastern and Central North America*, Donald Culross Peattie claims one tree is an astounding 240 feet tall. While that's likely an exaggeration, these pines are big—up to 42 inches in diameter and more than 200 years old. Hemlock, black birch, and northern red oak reach up to 250 years or more.

■ **DIRECTIONS**
Take I-91 north to Exit 13-Hanover-Norwich. Go east toward Hanover. Immediately after crossing the Connecticut River, turn left (north) onto River Road, which leads to Dartmouth's Ledyard Canoe Club. Drive to the last lot and park.

■ **HIGHLIGHTS**
Walk north and between the last two buildings on your left. Head to the right of the historic Tom Dent Cabin. The 0.75-mile trail is rough in places as it traverses a steep slope directly above the Connecticut River. Along the first section of the trail, the largest pines tower above. Soon they yield to a long stretch of ancient hemlock and black birch, which is then followed by a return of the soaring pines. Unusually luxuriant Canada yew decorates the slope, an indicator of lack of fire, deer, or other disturbance. At the steep dirt road on the right, you have arrived at the section that is officially called Pine Park. Follow the riverside trail to its end and return the way you came.

■ **CONTACT INFORMATION**
Dartmouth College Outdoor Programs, Robinson Hall, Hanover, New Hampshire 03755, 603-646-2428

110. Tamworth Big Pines

One of New England's best places to see white pines is at Tamworth Big Pines, formally known as the 108-acre Big Pines Natural Area of Hemenway State Forest. The striking mile-long stretch of road through it is the Northeast's version of California's Avenue of the Giants. One 54-inch-diameter giant reaches 149.8 feet, and numerous other pines are 125 to 145 feet tall, with diameters of up to 45 inches. At just 150 to 200 years of age, these behemoths still have not reached their maximum dimensions. Hemlocks, 250 to 350 years old, also grow here, along with sugar maple, red spruce, yellow birch, and red maple.

■ **DIRECTIONS**

Take I-93 north of Concord to Exit 24-Ashland. Go east on Routes 25 and 3, then drive east on Route 113 to North Sandwich. Take Route 113A to Hemenway State Forest on the right, and watch for a small pull-off on the right with a sign for Big Pines Natural Area.

■ **HIGHLIGHTS**

The half-mile nature trail starts next to the sign. It enters the Big Pines area and descends, crossing a bridge over the Swift River. Take a right on the Loop Trail up a hill, then later descend. The 54-inch-diameter giant is on the right of the trail. Be sure to wander off-trail to see the most impressive trees. Also check out the forest on the other side of the road, and head off-trail to find behemoth pines as large as 52 inches in diameter.

■ **CONTACT INFORMATION**

New Hampshire Division of Parks and Recreation, P.O. Box 1856, Concord, New Hampshire 03302, 603-271-3456 or 603-796-2323 (New Hampshire State Forest Nursery)

111. CHESTERFIELD GORGE

In the southwest corner of New Hampshire, 5-acre Chesterfield Gorge offers a pleasant surprise: 200-year-old hemlocks, 27 to 36 inches in diameter and 80 to 100 feet tall. A small waterfall adds to the charm of the gorge, which is popular during the summer.

■ **DIRECTIONS**

From I-91 in Vermont, go north of Brattleboro to Exit 3. Go east on Route 9 and cross the Connecticut River. Drive 8 miles to Chesterfield Gorge Natural Area, passing Spofford Lake on the left. The gorge is a mile beyond the town of Spofford. Parking is on the left.

■ **HIGHLIGHTS**

The only trail into the gorge descends steeply and brings you to the old growth in 0.2 mile, where it ends near the gorge bottom.

■ **CONTACT INFORMATION**

New Hampshire Division of Parks and Recreation, P.O. Box 1856, Concord, New Hampshire 03302, 603-271-3456

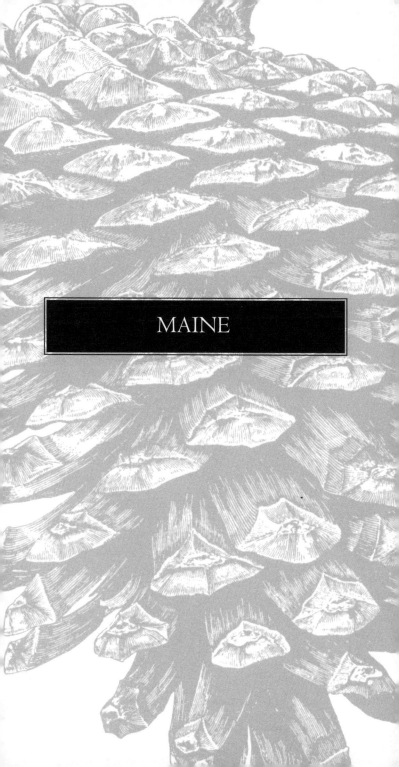

MAINE

Many people imagine Maine as the quintessential New England wilderness area. Striking photographs of heavy-antlered moose against the backdrop of rugged Mt. Katahdin call out to lovers of the wild. Famed philosopher Henry David Thoreau's descriptions of the Maine Woods conjure images of the virgin forests. The white pine, the official state tree, was once the most valuable timber tree in the world. One would expect to find New England's best old growth in the "Pine Tree State."

Unfortunately, the reverse is true. Maine's forests have been repeatedly cut over the years; today, timber and pulp companies own more than 90 percent of the state's forests. You're more likely to find large trees in Maine's city parks than in its wild areas.

Nonetheless, Maine still possesses worthwhile old-growth sites with considerable charms. What they lack in tree size, Maine's ancient stands make up for in character.

The incomparable Mt. Katahdin, where much of the state's old growth thrives, is perhaps the single most impressive mountain in the eastern United States. You're unlikely to get a more wild setting for old-growth viewing than in Maine.

Until the early 1990s, Maine's Critical Areas Program had the only modern old-growth inventory in the Northeast. This study tabulated 6,700 acres of big-tree old growth, with 5,000 acres in a single site—the Nature Conservancy's remote Big Reed Pond, which is also the largest contiguous old-growth site in New England. The remaining 1,700 big-tree acres are scattered among 82 sites, averaging only 20 acres per site. Other old growth in Maine likely includes forests of dwarf trees growing on upper mountain slopes (30,000 acres) and scattered old trees in peatlands and rocky barrens.

Most sites in Maine possess only modestly sized trees. The surviving stands of white pine and hemlock are smaller in stature than those found in the other New England states because of the state's aggressive logging history as well as its relatively brief growing season and severe winters.

However, there is reason for hope. We believe the final number of old-growth sites for Maine is likely to exceed 150, adding up to 1,000 acres to the currently recognized old growth in Maine.

112. BIG REED FOREST RESERVE

The last remnant of what philosopher Henry Thoreau called the "wildest country" in Maine is the 4,853-acre Big Reed Forest Reserve. As New England's largest ancient forest, it contains two-thirds of New England's old growth and is so pristine that the Nature Conservancy decided not to build trails or signs. Public visitation is by special arrangement only.

■ **HIGHLIGHTS**

Broadleaf forests of sugar maple up to 313 years old grow with 200-year-old beech and hop hornbeam. Hemlocks are the oldest, up to 436 years old. Balsam fir and red spruce that are more than 300 years old and up to 24 inches in diameter cover north slopes and steep rocky ridges. Nearly pure stands of 200-year-old northern white cedar grow along ponds. Other ancients include 150- to 200-year-old white ash, red maple, and yellow birch.

Rich growths of mosses and orchids decorate the forest floor. Especially notable is the diverse lichen population—more than 180 species, including 50 species that rarely grow anywhere except in ancient forests. An open sphagnum moss bog with insect-eating plants grows along 90-acre Big Reed Pond and 25-acre Little Reed Pond. Big Reed Pond is also home to blueback char, a state endangered fish found in only ten ponds on Earth.

Big Reed's old growth was long ignored because of its remote location and lack of many white pines. Fortunately, descendants of David Pingree, the timber baron who bought the forest in the mid-1800s, decided to preserve it. By 1990, they had sold it to the Nature Conservancy.

■ **CONTACT INFORMATION**

Open for guided tours only; contact for reservations and directions. The Nature Conservancy, Fort Andross, 14 Maine Street, Suite 401, Brunswick, Maine 04011, 207-729-5181

113. Mt. Katahdin and Basin Ponds

Maine's 5,267-foot Mt. Katahdin is the Northeast's tallest mountain, measured from base to summit, and also the closest in character to the Rockies. Its sharp, jagged peaks are connected by the spectacular 2-mile-long Knife Edge, which rises 3,000 feet and in some places is only 3 feet wide.

The mountain and neighboring Basin Ponds also feature five old-growth spruce stands totaling 942 acres. The most accessible are at Basin Ponds, where trees even up to 380 years old are relatively small because of the severe climate and 2,700-foot elevation.

Mt. Katahdin, famous as the northern terminus of the 2,700-mile-long Appalachian Trail, is part of one of America's largest state parks, 209,000-acre Baxter State Park. It boasts 4,000 acres of alpine tundra and, with neighboring peaks, 23,000 acres of never-logged subalpine dwarf balsam fir forest.

Hiking through these areas offers an experience of windswept desolation and pristine, rugged wilderness. Reaching the top of Mt. Katahdin requires a long, strenuous, steep hike permitted only during fair weather.

■ **DIRECTIONS**

From Bangor, Maine, take I-95 north 60 miles to Exit 56. Head west on Route 11. Upon leaving Millinocket, turn right on Golden Road. Follow signs to Baxter State Park. Turn right onto the park entrance road. Obtain a map. Drive to Roaring Brook Campground.

The best time to visit is in July or August. Inquire in advance about trail permits, which are limited on summer weekends. Camping permits require reservations months in advance.

From the campground, take the 5.3-mile round-trip Chimney Pond Trail. In 2 miles, pass Basin Ponds. Shortly after, turn right onto North Basin Cutoff Trail. Hike a half mile to where the trail begins to climb steeply. The ancient red spruce stand is on the north side abutting the trail.

To climb Mt. Katahdin and experience its virgin alpine zone, subalpine forests, and limitless vistas, you must consult a trail guide and get a permit far in advance. The challenging climb is 9.8 miles.

■ CONTACT INFORMATION

Baxter State Park, 64 Balsam Drive, Millinocket, Maine 04462, 207-723-5140

114. CATHEDRAL PINES OF EUSTIS

The 220-acre Cathedral Pines of Eustis showcases the Northeast's most impressive and accessible stand of old-growth red pine. More than 300 years old, they are among the oldest recorded in the United States, and their 35-inch diameters make them among the largest in the Northeast. These beautiful trees have large orange plates of bark similar to that of the western ponderosa pine. On a sunny day, these straight-as-an-arrow trees with their glowing bark are a sight to behold. The tallest soar to 118 feet.

Red pine is one of the Northeast's least common wild trees and, as an old-growth tree, is quite rare. Eustis is historically notable as one of the stops Benedict Arnold made on his ill-fated attempt to escape to Canada during the Revolutionary War.

■ **DIRECTIONS**

Take I-95 north from Augusta to alternate Route 202 north. Take Route 16 north, then Route 27 north to Eustis. About 32 miles from Kingfield, you pass between the orange aisles of red pines lining both sides of Route 27. Turn right into the entrance for Cathedral Pines Campground. Ask permission to drive or walk through the grounds to admire the pines.

■ **HIGHLIGHTS**

Walk along the campground loop road, which is lined with impressive pines. The campsites are also surrounded by their arching trunks. Then cross Route 27 opposite the campground entrance and take the nature loop trail through an ancient red pine forest. Visit during late afternoon to see the sun illuminate the trees.

■ **CONTACT INFORMATION**

Cathedral Pines Campground, Route 27 North, P.O. Box 146, Eustis, Maine 04936, 207-246-3491

115. HERMITAGE PRESERVE

Once a secluded cabin homestead, then an exclusive sportsmen's camp, and later a family camp, the 35-acre Hermitage Preserve offers the secluded beauty of its past to its visitors today. Five acres of the preserve harbor one of the last stands of large white pines in Maine.

The pines here reach 130 feet tall, up to 3 feet in diameter, and up to 200 years in age. They are the surviving remnant from the 1860s, when the original pines were logged.

In 1892, Campbell Young built a cabin under the pines, where he lived like a hermit for several years, giving the site its name. The Nature Conservancy purchased it in 1967 to protect the trees. A few years later, Congress designated it a National Natural Landmark.

■ DIRECTIONS

From Bangor, take I-95 north to Exit 54-Howland. Go west on Route 6 for 20 miles to Milo. Turn right on Route 11 and drive 12 miles. Turn left at the Katahdin Iron Works sign. Drive 7 miles to the Iron Works gate, register, and pay a fee. Proceed across the bridge and take the next right. Drive 7 miles on logging roads, crossing the West Branch of the Pleasant River near the halfway point. Note: logging trucks have the right-of-way. The parking lot is on your right.

■ HIGHLIGHTS

Follow the trail to the river crossing and the preserve on the other side. You can wade the river during most of the summer and fall.

To hike further into spectacular Gulf Hagas, which features five waterfalls and even more spectacular old growth, follow Gulf Hagas Trail west from the preserve. A mile later, reach the side trail to Screw Auger Falls. Three more falls are ahead.

■ CONTACT INFORMATION

The Nature Conservancy, Fort Andross, 14 Maine Street, Suite 401, Brunswick, Maine 04011, 207-729-5181

116. Old Blue Mountain

Some of the largest red spruce in Maine grow along hundreds of acres on the slopes of Old Blue Mountain, off a side trail of the Appalachian Trail.

The red spruce, usually a medium-sized tree, grow up to 75 feet here, with ages exceeding 310 years. The average diameter of 19 inches and the largest diameter of 28 inches are impressive for this species. Larger sugar maple and yellow birch also grow here.

■ **DIRECTIONS**

Take I-95 to Portland, then head north on Route 495 to Lewiston. From Exit 12, take Route 202 north into Auburn. Stay on Route 4 when Route 202 veers off to the right. In 17 miles, turn left onto Route 108 in Livermore. Proceed north and west for 22 miles. In Rumford, Route 108 crosses Androscoggin River. Turn right again on Route 120. Just before Andover, turn right (north) on South Arm Road and drive 8 miles. When you enter the deep Black Brook Notch, watch for the sign and trail blazes where the trail crosses the road. Park at the trailhead lot.

■ **HIGHLIGHTS**

This demanding but rewarding 10-mile hike climbs 2,300 feet. You can shorten it by 2.3 miles using one car at each end. To do this, drive up Route 5 and park the second car at the dirt road just after the brook at the 2.1-mile mark.

Take the marked trail north. Climb 900 feet up one of the steepest sections of this famous trail. At the top of the cliff, savor wonderful views. As the trail rises more gradually, you will walk through ancient red spruce and northern hardwood forest. Some trees, very old and impressive, have huge burl growths. Climb over four false summits and arrive at the base of Old Blue Mountain. You're rewarded with one of the best panoramic views in western Maine.

As you descend the mountain's north slope, the trees get larger and larger. After crossing a brook, you'll see huge red spruce trees of great age. Descend 600 feet to the saddle between Old Blue and Elephant Mountains and cross Clearwater Brook, going downstream. Decorating your route are delightful cascades and deep pools, glistening with gold flecks of iron pyrite.

You soon leave the brook and walk along an old woods road and arrive at Route 5. Turn left and walk 2.3 miles back to your car.

■ CONTACT INFORMATION

There is no property manager for this site.

117. Mt. Agamenticus

After more than 400 years of intensive logging, Mt. Agamenticus is one of the last places you would expect to find old-growth forest. Yet one old-growth sleuth recently discovered a 100-acre ancient forest on this mountain's slopes.

Large white pines between 200 and 300 years old grow with 200-year-old white oak and beech, 175-year-old black birch, and 150-year-old northern red oak. Hemlocks reach 30 inches in diameter. You can also find beautiful natural red pines, as thick as 20 inches, sugar maple, chestnut oak, red maple, yellow birch, and white ash.

Take Maine Turnpike (I-95) 7 miles north of New Hampshire's border, to Exit 1-York. Cross the bridge to the west side of the Maine Turnpike and turn right (north) on Chase's Pond Road. Drive 3 miles to Mountain Road and turn left (west) on Mountain Road. After 2.7 miles, look on your right for the driveway into the trail's gravel parking lot, just before the paved road ends. If you come to the service road to a fire tower, you passed the driveway.

■ HIGHLIGHTS

The 1-mile loop trail climbs 344 feet to the summit, passing through old growth. Climb the fire tower to the summit of 691-foot Mt. Agamenticus for exceptional views.

■ CONTACT INFORMATION

The Nature Conservancy, Fort Andross, 14 Maine Street, Suite 401, Brunswick, Maine 04011, 207-729-5181

118. BONNEY WOODS

With 88 percent of the state covered in trees, Maine is the most forested state in the nation. But most of Maine's remote woods are decidedly industrial, intensely managed "pulp and paper" lands. Most of Maine's ancient groves are next to villages and cities. Twenty-acre Bonney Woods, surrounded by the village of Farmington, is one such example.

The preserve's outstanding features are its large, towering hemlocks, along with ancient yellow birch, beech, sugar and red maple, and white ash. Ages range from 150 to 350 years, diameters are up to 43 inches, and heights are as much as 115 feet.

■ **DIRECTIONS**

Take I-95 to Augusta to Exit 31. Follow Route 27 north for 33 miles into Farmington. Turn right onto Route 4 and head north a short distance. At Franklin County Court House, turn right onto Anson Street. Drive a quarter mile, watching for the Bonney Woods sign at a small parking area on the right.

■ **HIGHLIGHTS**

Walk the main trail through the grove. Also make sure to check out the short side trails, including one that ends at the Anson Cemetery, which has gravestones dating back to 1819.

■ **CONTACT INFORMATION**

Bonney Woods Corporation, 204 Anson Street, Farmington, Maine 04938, 207-778-3495

119. BOWDOIN PINES

As one of the oldest forests on the coast of Maine, Bowdoin Pines, appropriately, are part of the oldest college in Maine, Bowdoin College (founded in 1794). (It's also appropriate that Bowdoin College is the alma mater of America's "poet of primeval forests," Henry Wadsworth Longfellow.) The 33-acre preserve is part of the original 200-acre gift to the college from the Town of Brunswick in 1791.

These statuesque 40-inch-thick white pines, which reach and may exceed 120 feet in height, reportedly originated on eighteenth-century farmland 150 to 200 years ago. Secondary old-growth hemlock grow up to 30 inches in diameter. Other old trees include yellow birch, red spruce, sugar maple, and northern red oak.

■ **DIRECTIONS**

Take Maine Turnpike to Exit 9, then I-95 to Exit 22. Take Route 1 into Brunswick and turn right on Maine Street. Turn left onto Bath Road at a large, white church on the corner. Pass the Federal Street traffic light and turn left into a driveway to a parking lot only 100 yards farther. Alternate parking is on Federal Street.

■ **HIGHLIGHTS**

At the trailhead, take the right-hand fork. The tallest and largest pines are along the first half of the trail loop. Follow the 0.7-mile trail around the perimeter of the preserve.

■ **CONTACT INFORMATION**

Bowdoin College, Brunswick, Maine 04011, 207-725-3253

120. Ordway Pines

Ordway Pines could easily earn the distinction of being the greatest living symbol of Maine. It claims the tallest tree in the state—an eastern white pine—which is the official state tree and the centerpiece of Maine's flag. Ordway Pines is also the state's tallest forest.

■ DIRECTIONS

Take Maine Turnpike north of Portland to Exit 11. Turn east on Routes 4 and 202. Immediately after Route 100 joins your road, turn left onto Route 26 north. In 27 miles, in downtown Norway, turn left (west) on Route 117 (Main Street). Turn right on Danforth Street. Town Hall is on the right. Ask for a brochure and directions at the service window.

* HIGHLIGHTS

The champion of this 9-acre grove is 155 feet tall. Many others are 140 to 149 feet and have diameters of 30 to 40 inches or more. Their ages are between 200 and 350 years. Ancient 36-inch-diameter northern red oak, as well as ancient hemlock and beech, also grow here.

This virgin old-growth grove is one of the earliest ancient forests in Maine to be protected. In 1930, a forestry report documented seventy-three white pines and hemlocks in the grove. The Twin Towns Nature Club saved it from logging and has owned it since 1931.

■ CONTACT INFORMATION

Town of Norway, 19 Danforth Street, Norway, Maine 04268, 207-743-6651

121. Waldoboro Town Forest

The second oldest hemlock site inventoried in Maine is the 5-acre ancient forest portion of Waldoboro Town Forest. The largest hemlocks reach up to 41 inches in diameter, and the largest yellow birth reach up to 27 inches. Trees range in age from 170 to 240 years. The hemlock–yellow birch–red maple combination makes this site highly unusual for Maine. Other trees include white pine, red spruce, sugar maple, and paper birch.

■ **DIRECTIONS**

Take I-95 to Exit 22-Brunswick, then Route 1 north through Brunswick for about 48 miles toward Waldoboro. When you see the "Entering Waldoboro" sign, immediately pull into the dirt parking lot on the left.

■ **HIGHLIGHTS**

To find the trail, face west, with the forest to your left. Walk 100 feet west along the edge of the woods to the road that enters the town forest. Follow the woods road into the old growth for a quarter mile. When the old growth ends, return by walking off-trail through the woods to the left, paralleling the trail. You will get to see even larger trees.

■ **CONTACT INFORMATION**

Town of Waldoboro, P.O. Box J, Waldoboro, Maine 04572, 207-832-5369

How Much Old Growth
Is in the Northeast?

An estimated 440,000 acres of ancient forest survive in the Northeast.* While this sounds like a large amount, it represents only 0.64 of 1 percent of the region's total forest land. Further, only a small portion of that acreage, less than 25 percent, is big-tree old growth; the rest is composed of small but ancient trees on poor habitats. About 68 percent (300,000 acres) is in northern New York's Adirondack State Forest Preserve, although there are a few sizeable patches elsewhere, including the Catskills (70,000 acres of subalpine dwarf forest), Big Reed Pond Preserve in Maine (4,853 acres), Allegheny National Forest in Pennsylvania (3,320 acres), Ricketts Glen State Park in Pennsylvania (2,000 acres), Cook Forest State Park in Pennsylvania (1,300 acres), and Green Lakes State Park (1,000 acres). While there are other sizeable parcels in the range of hundreds of acres, most of the rest exists in relatively small slivers of 4 to 80 acres. The average size outside the Adirondacks is only 20 acres.

In the following table, the amount of acreage is based on how well each state has been explored and surveyed. Massachusetts, western New York, and the Adirondacks are the most studied, while New Jersey, central New York, New Hampshire, Vermont, and Maine have been only lightly surveyed. Undoubtedly, more old-growth sites exist but have not been discovered or have not been reported.

*This figure is the sum of all known old-growth acreage in each Northeastern state. However, because the numbers are estimates and most state surveys are incomplete, the actual figure is likely between 420,000 and 540,000 acres.

STATE	# OF SITES	ACREAGE OF ALL OLD GROWTH*	% OF STATE'S OLD GROWTH
New York (minus Adirondack/Catskill Forest Preserve lands)	110	5,000	0.02 %
Adirondacks	50+	*300,000+	
Catskills	20+	70,000+	
Pennsylvania	52	~10,000	0.06 %
New Jersey	16	670	0.03 %
Connecticut	10	200	0.01 %
Rhode Island	3	50+	0.01 %
Massachusetts	55	3,700+	0.07 %
Vermont	55	2,100+	0.05 %
New Hampshire	33	~20,000 **	0.41 %
Maine	26	~30,000 **	0.17 %
Total Number of Sites: 430+			
Subtotal (minus Adirondacks/Catskills)		~67,000+	0.10 %
Total		**~442,000+**	**0.64 %**

* Estimates range from 150,000 to 500,000 acres of Adirondacks old growth, no more than 30 to 40 percent of which is big-tree old growth. We settled on 300,000 acres of total old growth for this book, but more research is needed for an accurate figure.
** Acreage includes small-stature forest of wetlands and upper mountain slopes. Big-tree old growth-only totals are: New York = roughly 120,000 acres (0.70%); Vermont = 1,100 acres (0.025%); New Hampshire = 2,200 acres (0.04%); Maine = less than 6,700 acres (0.03%).

Source: *Old Growth in the East* (a 1993 inventory by Mary Byrd Davis), with supplemental data collected by the authors.

Oldest Tree Champions by Species

Source: Records of Dr. Charles Cogbill, Bruce Kershner, and Robert Leverett

CONIFER TREE

SPECIES	AGE (YEARS)	LOCATION
No. white cedar	1,693	near Toronto, Ontario, Niagara escarpment
	510	Niagara Gorge, NY-Ontario border
Eastern hemlock	998	Ricketts Glen State Park old growth, PA
	607	Tionesta Natural Area old growth, PA
	600	Alan Seeger Natural Area old growth, PA
	~500	several sites, western NY
White spruce	636	northern tree line, NW Territories, Canada
	249	Gaspe Peninsula, Quebec
Black spruce	504	Ungava Peninsula, northern Quebec
	363	dwarf, Mt. Washington summit, NH
Eastern white pine	492	Michigan
	460	Nelson Swamp, near Syracuse, NY
Red spruce	426	New Hampshire, Maine
Red pine	360	Ontario
Pitch pine	352	high cliffs, Minnewaska State Park, NY
	220	Old Maids Woods, Schenectady, NY
	220	Taconic Mountains, MA
Tamarack	335	Isle Royale National Park, MI
Balsam fir	220	Labrador, Newfoundland

BROADLEAF TREE

SPECIES	AGE (YEARS)	LOCATION
Black gum	679	New Hampshire
	550	Backus Woods old growth, southern Ontario
	520	Oakham, MA
	~480	Bear Swamp old growth, NJ
Black gum	435	Vernon Swamp old growth, VT
	~400	Tiffany Brook Preserve, Long Island
Tulip tree	600	North Carolina
	435	Several locations in Northeast
American sycamore	500	Sunderland, MA
American elm	500	Marietta, OH
Sugar maple	440	Huron Mountain, MI
	420	Tionesta Natural Area, PA
Bur oak	440	Ohio

BROADLEAF TREE (CONT.)

SPECIES	AGE (YEARS)	LOCATION
Yellow birch	436	Ampersand Mountain old growth, Adirondacks, NY
		Laurentian Highlands, Quebec
	369	Wachusett Mountain, MA
White oak	426	Buckaloons State Park, Warren, PA
American beech	412	Tionesta old growth, PA
	329	Heart's Content old growth, PA
Chestnut oak	398	Great Smokies, TN
	376	Tionesta old growth, PA
Black birch	330	Upper Peninsula, MI
Pignut hickory	330	Great Smokies National Park, TN
Northern red oak	322	Wachusett Mountain, MA
White ash	310	Joyce Kilmer Natural Area,
		Nantahala National Forest, NC
Paper birch (lowland var.)	302	Schibougamu, Quebec
Paper birch (mountain var.)	232	Nancy Brook, NH
E. cottonwood	~300	Balmville, NY
	214	Reinstein Woods Nature Preserve, NY
Cucumber magnolia	300	Heart's Content, PA
Red maple	287	Heart's Content, PA
Shagbark hickory	275	Dick Cove Natural Area, TN
Black ash	264	Hay Creek, MN
Black cherry	258	Tionesta Natural Area, PA
American holly	225	Sunken Forest,
		Fire Island National Seashore, NY
Hop hornbeam	251	Big Reed Reserve, ME

Tallest and Largest Tree Champions by Species

Source: Records of Eastern Native Tree Society (for forest-grown records) and National Register of Big Trees, 2002-2003 (American Forests) (for open-grown records)

TALLEST TREE RECORDED (FEET)		
TREE SPECIES	NORTHEAST	ENTIRE RANGE
Eastern white pine	180.9	207
Tulip tree	156	175.5
Eastern hemlock	143.9	169.8
White ash	157.4	164
American sycamore	155	159
Sweet gum	100 +	157.1
Bitternut hickory	136.4	154.1
Red spruce	129.2	152
Sugar maple	138	151
White oak	124.8	147.8
Black cherry	137	146
Cucumber magnolia	122.9	145
Chestnut oak	111.1	144.4
Northern red oak	130.9	144.4
Red pine	118.8	143.6
Eastern cottonwood	133.1	134.6
Shagbark hickory	131.7	131.7
American basswood	128.7	128.7
Red maple	126	145
Slippery (red) elm	120.4	141.2
Black birch	116.2	117
Yellow birch	104	110

LARGEST CIRCUMFERENCE OF TRUNK RECORDED (FEET)

| NORTHEAST | | ENTIRE RANGE | |
(FOREST GROWN)*	(FIELD GROWN)*	(FOREST GROWN)	(FIELD GROWN)
15	16	16	18
16	24	25	31
15	n/a	19	n/a
14	25	14	25
15	21	17	37
11	16	16	23
11	n/a	14	15
10	n/a	14	n/a
15	21	16	23
14	25	20	32
13	17	17	18
13	21	18	24
14	18	18	18
18	24	22	34
10	n/a	12	n/a
18	22	19	36
12	12	15	15
14	24	13	23
18	20	23	23
51	8	21	n/a
10	15	13	15
15	21	16	21

* Trees that grow in forests typically develop much narrower trunks than those that grow in open fields, because there is much less light in forests. Field-grown trees quickly develop thick trunks with low, open, spreading boughs in the abundant light. Champion tree lists are heavily biased toward listing open-grown trees that don't grow in natural forest habitats. Therefore, largest tree sizes in natural forests are widely underreported in popular champion lists.

Resources for More Information on Northeastern Old-Growth Forest

BOOKS

The Catskill Forest: A History, by Michael Kudish. 2000. Purple Mountain Press, 217 pp.

The Cook Forest, an Island in Time, by Anthony E. Cook. 1997. Falcon Publishing, 96 pp.

Eastern Old-Growth Forests: Prospects for Rediscovery and Recovery, edited by Mary Byrd Davis. 1996. Island Press, 383 pp.

The Great Forest of the Adirondacks, by Barbara McMartin. 1994. North Country Press, 240 pp.

Guide to Ancient Forests of Zoar Valley Canyon, by Bruce Kershner. 2001. New York Old Growth Forest Association and Citizens Campaign for the Environment, 52 pp.

National Register of Big Trees: 2002-2003. American Forests, 48 pp. (P.O. Box 2000, Washington, D.C. 20013, 800-545-TREE.)

Old Growth in the East: A Survey, by Mary Byrd Davis. 1993. Wild Earth Publications. 150 pp.

Western New York Old Growth Forest Survey: Preliminary Report, by Bruce Kershner. 1995. Western New York Survey Team, 127 pp.

ORGANIZATIONS AND AGENCIES

American Forests, P.O. Box 2000, Washington D.C. 20013, 800-545-TREE, www.americanforests.org/resources/bigtrees

Big Trees of Massachusetts,
   www.massforesters.org/bigtrees.htm

Connecticut Notable Trees Project,
   www.conncoll.edu/ccrec/greennet/ct.trees

Cook Forest State Park, P.O. Box 120, Cooksburg, Pennsylvania
   16217, 814-744-8407, cookforestsp@state.pa.us

Eastern Native Tree Society, 52 Fairfield Ave., Holyoke, Massachusetts 01040, www.uark.edu/misc/ents, or dbhguru@attbi.com

Eastern Old Growth Clearinghouse, P.O. Box 131, Georgetown,
   Kentucky 40324, www.old-growth.org

New Jersey's Big Tree Program,
   www.nj.gov/dep/parksandforests/forest/community/
   bigtree.html

Lists of New York old-growth forests,
   www.championtrees.org/oldgrowth/index.htm (click on "New
   York")

New York State Big Tree Register,
   www.dec.state.ny.us/website/dlf/privland/urban/bigtree.html

Pennsylvania State Park Big Tree Program,
   www.dcnr.state.pa.us/stateparks/natural/bigtree.htm

Vermont Tree Society, 9 Langdon Street #3, Montpelier, Vermont
   05602, info@vermonttreesociety.org or 802-223-6275,
   www.vermonttreesociety.org

Wild Earth, P.O. Box 455, Richmond, Vermont 05477, 802-434-
   4077, info@wildlandsproject.org

Index